The Worldview of
Saint Augustine

The Worldview of Saint Augustine

Written by
Evgeny Nikolayevitch Trubetskoy

Translated by
Filip Poutintsev

Original Russian edition published in 1892:
Миросозерцание Блаженного Августина
Трубецкой Евгений Николаевич

ISBN: 9798268498721

Publisher: Filip Poutintsev
poutintsev.com
filip@poutintsev.com

Translation and Introduction: Filip Poutintsev

Copyright © 2025 Filip Poutintsev. All rights reserved.

Cover art: *St. Augustine and the Mystery of the Trinity*
by Pinturicchio (Bernardino di Betto), 1495-1496
Cover design: Filip Poutintsev

Table on Contents

Introduction 6
Part: I 8
    Chapter: I 8
    Chapter: II 23
    Chapter: III 35
Part: I 64
    Chapter: I 64
    Chapter: II 73
    Chapter: III 81
    Chapter: IV 96

Introduction

Saint Augustine, also known as Augustine of Hippo, with his Latin name Aurelius Augustinus Hipponensis (354–430 A.D.), was a Roman philosopher, theologian, and bishop who profoundly influenced Western Christianity and philosophy. He is renowned for his writings on faith, reason, and politics, including The City of God and Confessions. Initially leading a non-Christian life, he later found faith, was baptized, and became a prominent figure in the Roman Catholic Church.

In this book, Trubetskoy presents a profound study of St. Augustine as the apologist of the theocratic ideal of Western Christianity. Trubetskoy traces Augustine's intellectual journey – from his struggle with Manichaean dualism, through his defense of the unity of the Church against Donatism, to his decisive battle with Pelagianism over the meaning of grace and freedom. Against the backdrop of Rome's decline and the rise of the barbarian world, Augustine's vision of the Civitas Dei emerges as a response to the crisis of civilization: a universal divine order that transcends the collapse of the earthly empire. Trubetskoy shows Augustine not only as a Father of the Church, but as the thinker who laid the foundations of medieval Catholicism, with all its strengths and contradictions. In his analysis, he reveals the depth of Augustine's religious genius, his passion for truth, his longing for God – and the tensions between his personal faith and the Latin system that history compelled him to defend.

Evgeny Nikolayevich Trubetskoy (1863–1920) was a Russian philosopher of the Tsarist era, a jurist, and a religious and social figure; professor at the Universities of Kyiv (1897–1905) and Moscow (1905–1917). His father was the musicologist Nikolai Petrovich Trubetskoy, one of the founding members of the Moscow Conservatory, and his brother was another famous philosopher of that time, Sergei Nikolaevich Trubetskoy. Their family was an influential noble house formed in the 14th century, descending from the grandson of Gediminas (1275–1341), Grand Duke of Lithuania.

After the Revolution, the Trubetskoy family, along with other noble families, opposed the Bolsheviks and supported the White Army. However, when the Red Army prevailed, most of them, including his son, the philosopher and writer Sergei Evgenievich Trubetskoy, emigrated to France. Evgeny himself did not make it, as he died during the Civil War in 1920 of typhus.

PART: 1

The Worldview of Saint Augustine

CHAPTER: I

The fifth century is undoubtedly one of the most significant epochs in Christian civilization. It is a critical age when the Church, fully armed with a mature organization, enters the Middle Ages, handing itself over from the ancient Greco-Latin world to the barbarians while also absorbing elements of the Greco-Latin tradition. At the same time, this is the century when the distinction between Hellenic (Eastern) and Latin (Western) Christianity becomes sharply and distinctly apparent.

The political order of that time was shaken at its very foundations; only the Church represented social unity, holding together the Empire, which was falling apart in the process of self-disintegration. Alone, it resisted separatist movements and centrifugal forces that threatened the state with destruction. Against the barbarians, breaking through the weakened legions on all sides, the Church alone embodied the cultural unity of the Greco-Latin world.

"Amid the storms of the world," said St. Ambrose of Milan at the end of the 4th century, "the Church remains unmoved; the waves break upon her without being able to shake her. While all around her resounds a terrible crash, she alone offers a quiet haven to all shipwrecked souls, where they may find salvation."

At that time, the Church was not only a spiritual but also a worldly unity. The enfeebled state was unable to perform its most elementary functions. Secular power could no longer defend the state by its own strength from without or bind it from within. It provided neither just courts nor tolerable administration. Thus, the Church, as the only living force in society, was compelled, willingly or unwillingly, to take on secular affairs and perform the tasks of state power. In that epoch, we see bishops acting as civil administrators and judges, resolving inheritance disputes and similar matters, and also serving as diplomats.

In those harsh times, necessity sometimes even forced them to take an active part in military defense: in besieged cities, the bishop often stood at the head of the defense. In both the East and the West, the Church saved the state by fulfilling its functions. This led to the formation of an order in which ecclesiastical unity was intertwined with state unity, where the order of grace was not sharply distinguished from the worldly order. Constantine the Great understood that the Empire could not, by its own strength alone, withstand the natural process of decay and death. Knowing the state could not save itself, could not stand upon the material basis of mere power and military might, he sought a supernatural foundation for it and called upon the Church to support Rome. He wished to hold the state together through a unified Church. For this very reason, he and his successors sought to occupy the head of the Church, ruling the state through it.

On the one hand, the emperor sought to make his secular authority the center of Christian society, subordinating spiritual authority as a mere instrument of his power. On the other hand, the Church possessed an impulse toward independence, and the attempts of Eastern emperors to assume supremacy in matters of faith met vigorous resistance. Against the claims of secular power stood the independent episcopate, with the bishop of Rome as its head and center.

In both the East and the West during this period, we see the formation of a peculiar Christian theocracy, where Church and state were intertwined. They did not merge into a single whole, but clear and fixed boundaries between them did not exist. In both halves of the Empire, this blending of ecclesiastical and political spheres led, however, to opposite results. In the East, one unchanging principle of ecclesiastical policy runs like a red thread through all the reigns of Christian emperors, immortalized by Emperor Constantius in the classical phrase he spoke to the council of bishops in Milan: "What I will, let that be your canon." For him, one canon and especially one dogma represented not only one Church but also one state. Thus, in questions of dogma, the emperor was interested not only as a believer but also as the representative of worldly power. From Constantine's point of view, as inherited by his successors, it was necessary to preserve the unity of the state by establishing one God and one faith. From this perspective, any dogmatic dispute or division in the Church appeared as a threat to the integrity of the state. To maintain power, it was necessary to compel subjects to believe as the emperor believed; whoever held a different confession was not only a heretic but also a rebel. Hence, the emperor's aspiration to determine the very content of Christian dogma. He assumed the functions of spiritual authority, dictating to his subjects dogmatic formulas: to believe or not to believe in the consubstantiality of the Son with the Father, in the equality of the Holy Spirit with the Son, to acknowledge one or two natures in Christ, and so forth. Emperors, whether heretical or orthodox, acted in this way. And if the Church was entrusted with diverse secular tasks, the emperor strove all the more to assert supremacy over it, turning it into an organ of his temporal policy.

Of course, the emperors' ambition was not the sole cause of such an order. In the eyes of the Christian masses, the emperor was the defender of the faith, the center of Christian society, and therefore the master of the Church. Bishops themselves appealed to him to resolve their dogmatic disputes, and, as often happens, those who managed to win him over acknowledged his right to authoritative intervention in matters of faith, while those against whom his power turned denied that right. If, on the one hand, the emperor sought supremacy in faith, on the other, the hierarchy sought to transform dogmas into binding legal norms. The pagan past of the Empire, where no separate priestly class had existed and any magistrate could perform priestly functions, had not prepared society to distinguish between spiritual and secular orders; thus, we see them interwoven and mingled even in the Christian Empire.

In the East, where secular power was relatively strong, this mingling led to the predominance of secular authority, which usurped the Church's functions. In the West, the situation was entirely different. Throughout the 4th and 5th centuries, down to the fall of the Western Empire, we see a steady decline of secular authority on the one hand, and on the other a rapid growth and strengthening of an independent episcopate. Developing swiftly, spiritual authority here dominated the secular sphere, eventually subordinating even imperial power itself. A complex set of cultural and historical conditions has produced this difference between the West and the East.

In the West, the Christian Empire never had solid ground beneath its feet and was doomed to impotence from the beginning. By moving his residence to the East, Constantine recognized that he could not break the traditions of pagan Rome and dreamed only of escaping them himself. Pagans at that time formed the majority in the West, and in Rome, they remained the ruling force. The Senate was filled with pagans. Rome remained the center of paganism, and not even Constantine could engage in open battle with it. The Christian Empire could not abolish the pagan order but could exist only alongside it as another Rome, the city of Constantine. As head of Christianity in the East, Constantine remained head of paganism in the West. As an external high priest in Constantinople, he did not cease to be the supreme pontiff in Rome. If in the East his paganism was ignored, in the West his Christianity was ignored. Officially, the Empire in the West did not cease to be pagan, whereas in the East, it had already become Christian.

Throughout the 4th century, pagans in Rome remained a formidable force, if not a majority, and through their silent opposition, they paralyzed the authority of the Christian emperor. This alone doomed Western Caesars to impotence. The pagan majority regarded them with hostility or indifference; their only support was the Christian minority. In this divided society, they stood between two fires: they feared angering the pagans with harsh measures and did not dare wage an energetic and consistent struggle against them. Yet, by neutrality or excessive indecision, by passivity toward the pagans, they risked alienating the Christians.

As already noted, they had no solid ground beneath their feet, and the Christian element on which they relied kept them dependent upon it. In contrast to the direct and consistent internal policy of the Eastern emperors, the policy of the Western Caesars strikes us by its frequent vacillations and its lack of any consistent principle. Constantius, for example, while ruling over both halves of the Empire, could voice the same claims in the West and enforce them with the same despotic methods as in the East. However, his successor, Valentinian, did not strive for supremacy in matters of faith; instead, he maintained a neutral policy toward all religious views, including both Christian and pagan ones. Gratian, on the other hand, submitted entirely to the guidance of Ambrose, bishop of Milan, bowing in his person before the authoritative leadership of the Church. The very circumstance that created weakness in the emperors of the West produced strength in the Church.

From the beginning, Christian emperors were unable to reside in Rome, the center of pagan opposition. Pagans held the chief civil magistracies. The pagan party, in order to preserve the former significance of its cult, was obliged to pretend that no change had occurred, that everything remained as before. Indeed, emperors continued to be proclaimed divine after their deaths, and the Senate established official cults in their honor. A Christian Caesar could not sanction such a state of affairs by his presence. At the same time, he dared not openly oppose it, for that would have meant provoking a powerful pagan party against himself. To avoid this fatal conflict, emperors seldom appeared in Rome, instead residing in Milan or Ravenna, drawn there by the necessity of being closer to the northern frontier, which was constantly threatened by barbarian invasions. They allowed themselves to be worshipped from afar and turned a blind eye to the abnormal state of affairs, which they could not change. But as a result, Rome, the political center of their realm, slipped out of their sphere of influence. The Christian community, with its bishop at its head, stood alone there against the kingdom of paganism, carrying the struggle with paganism upon its own shoulders without support from the state. The authority of the emperor was thereby annihilated: as a Christian, he was powerless over his pagan subjects; as the object of pagan cult and as supreme pontiff, he was nothing in the eyes of Christians.

The significance of the episcopate grew in proportion to the decline of imperial authority, and especially the role of the Roman bishop, the pope, increased. The capital of the ancient world inevitably became the focal point of the struggle between Christianity and paganism. Bearing this struggle on its own, the Roman Church became accustomed to independence and enjoyed a freedom that no other Church in the Empire possessed. To a great extent, this gave rise to a self-sufficient and independent spiritual authority, unknown in the East, where the Caesar posed as representative of Christian unity and dominated the majority of the episcopate.

In Rome, in the eyes of most pagans who stood on the ground of the Empire's centuries-old traditions, the emperor's Christianity was a mere accident. At the same time, Christians likewise were unaccustomed to regarding him as their active ally. The representative of Christian unity here was the pope, not the emperor. For Roman Christians, the pope was greater than the Caesar: the latter had no power over him and could not compel him to submit. Even in pagan times, the Roman community, with its bishop, had acquired preeminent importance in the eyes of Christians as the center of the struggle against paganism.

Rome held a special status as the place where representatives of all parts of the Empire, of all nationalities, and therefore of all Christian communities, came together. Thus, here more clearly than anywhere else, the universal, catholic character of the Church was expressed. Rome was the center of human communion, not bound to any particular locality or nationality, and therefore the center of Christian communion. In the Christian Empire, everything favored the strengthening of this universal significance of the Roman community and of the Roman bishop, especially the weak and ambiguous policy of the Western Caesars. Passing out of the sphere of imperial influence, Christian Rome became the papal city of Rome. It ceased to be a secular capital and was established instead as the city of

St. Peter and the seat of the apostolic see.

This was further advanced by the fact that the Roman Emperor was preoccupied with the task of preserving the Empire's frontiers and unity intact. His gaze was constantly turned north or south: in Gaul, he was threatened now by barbarian invasion, now by the revolt of legions under a usurper's banner. Africa, the granary of the Empire, posed another danger, for any uprising there would cut off the grain supply and cause famine in Italy. Torn between the far north and the far south of his domains, the emperor let slip from his grasp the center of his state, unwittingly yielding it to the fast-growing influence of the pope. Pressed everywhere by external enemies and separatist movements, he was compelled to turn to the Church, the only force that in that age bound society together, uniting men while everything else divided them. His strength was the Church's strength, but for that very reason, he had to heed its authoritative voice and inevitably submit to it. Already at the end of the fourth century, even the bishop of Milan, Ambrose, not the pope, could command emperors.

As secular authority weakened, sinking into senile impotence, the spiritual authority of the bishop stepped into its place, fulfilling its functions. Augustine complained that, as bishop, he was so overwhelmed with secular and civil affairs that they hindered his pastoral duties. The mingling of Church and state, which in the East had taken the form of secular despotism – state domination over the Church – led to the opposite result in the West: the state gradually withdrew from the Church, while the Church gradually assumed the state. The rise of the bishops over the state was also aided by the noble role they played during the barbarian invasions. At a moment when the state was powerless to save its subjects from the fury of conquerors, bishops acted as protectors of the civilian population. They assumed the role of mediators between victors and vanquished, doing what the state could not – saving their defenseless flock by restraining the wild, destructive instincts of the barbarians. Naturally, Christians placed their hopes more in their bishops, expecting salvation from them rather than from secular power.

The Eastern emperors, through their caesaropapist ambitions, also indirectly contributed to the expansion of papal power, albeit in a purely spiritual sphere. To a large extent, thanks to them, the pope's influence extended far beyond the Western Empire, reaching the distant East. By spreading their religious convictions through threats and violence, Eastern emperors sought to make their creed a universal compulsory norm, persecuting dissenters as rebels against their authority. Hence, whenever a heretical Caesar sat on the Constantinopolitan throne, the orthodox churches of the East, harassed and oppressed by him, looked for support and aid from outside. Naturally, their eyes turned to the center of independent ecclesiastical authority – Rome. Appealing to the Roman bishop as the supreme authority in the Christian world, they usually acknowledged him as the highest authority and judge in their disputes during troubled times. Imperial heresies always worked to the advantage of the popes, allowing them to appear as defenders of persecuted orthodoxy and as representatives of the universal Church, embracing both the West and the East in its unity. By their intolerant policies, Eastern emperors strengthened papal influence, drawing Eastern Orthodox churches into their sphere of influence. Thus, the influence, and in part the authority, of the pope extended beyond the Western Empire.

In times of peace and security, this authority was generally not recognized in the East; however, during periods of persecution and critical moments in Church life, it was invoked and could not be dispensed with. Against the weak and insignificant imperial authority in the West, by the end of the 4th century, there already stood a mighty spiritual power of universal influence and significance. One may say that here the

Church alone held together and upheld a state on the verge of collapse. In the East, the Church stood under the protection of the state. In the West, it was left to itself. More than that, it guarded and sustained state power itself in the persons of feeble and powerless emperors.

Looking closely at this epoch, we see that by the end of the 4th and the beginning of the 5th century, all the elements of medieval life and the marks of European civilization were already present. The atomized individualism of a disintegrating society was already blending with the individualism of the incoming Germanic elements breaking into the Empire. The political order, shaken to its foundation, was no longer able to restrain anarchic arbitrariness, and the Church alone stood against the individualized person with his striving for boundless freedom and insatiable thirst for life. Accustomed to a varied range of practical activities, both spiritual and secular, the Church gradually absorbed elements of ancient culture and imbibed the state ideals of ancient Rome. Its bishops appeared not only as representatives of spiritual authority but also of secular traditions, including legal and administrative ones. Its clergy, in ruling and governing men, could serve the barbarians not only as teachers of faith but also as teachers of law.

On this ground grew and developed the theocratic ideal which, already at the beginning of the 5th century, found its classical expression in the works of Blessed Augustine. It is of him that we shall now speak.

CHAPTER: II

Blessed Augustine is one of the most fascinating figures in history. To assess him is one of the most challenging tasks, given the diversity and richness of the elements that entered into his teaching and that shaped his character in various ways. Augustine embodies, in every respect, the transitional age of the fifth century, when one decrepit world was collapsing and another was being built upon its ruins.

He stands at the boundary between antiquity and the Middle Ages: while gathering the fragments of ancient culture, he simultaneously laid the foundations of medieval thought, and in part, even modern European thought. In the words of Charpentier, Augustine's Civitas Dei is "the funeral oration of the old world and the prophetic announcement of the new." These words can serve as a fitting characterization of his entire life and work. In every respect, his personality is twofold: within him were embodied and concentrated all the contradictions of his age. More than that, he anticipated and united in himself the contrasts of later times, for while he was the father and, one might say, the founder of medieval Catholicism, other aspects of his teaching simultaneously made him a prophet of Protestantism.

And if Protestants and Catholics alike see in him their progenitor, then without hesitation we may recognize him as the father of Western Christianity in all its main branches.

The son of a dissolute African pagan father and a Christian saint, Augustine remained throughout his life a dual product of paganism and Christianity, which contended within him to the very end without ever wholly overcoming one another. His inner struggle was a world struggle, and the process of psychological development which he immortalized in his Confessions is a vivid image of that world crisis. The two opposite states of mind that succeeded each other in Augustine's life – unbridled paganism in his youth and holy Christianity in his mature years – corresponded to two social environments; his inner division reflected the division of society at large.

Augustine's native land, North Africa, offers a striking example of such a divided society. Here, opposite tendencies were intensified by the passionate and impressionable African temperament. Africa in this epoch was a land of contrasts: extreme asceticism side by side with the crudest licentiousness, tribal religiosity alongside every form of sensual excess.

A younger contemporary of Augustine, Salvian, described Africa as if it were one great house of vice: a chaste African, he said, was no African at all. It was a land of the most horrific unnatural vices. One could hardly walk the streets of Carthage, the African capital, he said, without being defiled. And yet Africa was also the homeland of such great teachers of the Church as Tertullian, of saints such as the martyr Cyprian, and of Augustine himself. Salvian was horrified at the irreligion of African society, including even the Christians, who mingled Christian worship with pagan rites, offering sacrifices to idols and then approaching Christian altars.

A characteristic trait of the Africans was their hatred of monks and ascetics. A monk who entered Carthage by chance was met with curses, mockery, and insults. The apostles, says Salvian, could enter pagan cities with more safety than monks could enter Christian Carthage. Society, as this description shows, was torn between the asceticism of solitary hermits, driven into the desert by general hatred, and the unrestrained debauchery of the masses. Salvian's severity tends somewhat toward exaggeration, and Gaston Boissier rightly warns against relying on his testimony too uncritically. But in this case, we have no reason to doubt his words, since we derive the same impression from Augustine's own writings, especially the Confessions: here too we see a frenzied, corrupt society forming the dark background against which such exceptional figures as Saint Monica stand out in bold relief.

Thus, the polar opposition in Augustine's moods corresponded to the polar opposition in the society of his time. What were the main impressions of his life? On one side, a multitude of morally fallen people; on the other, a few saints, select personalities. On one side, discredited cults and wild orgies of a dying old religion; on the other, Christianity, the only force that gave its followers strength to maintain moral elevation.

Within himself, Augustine experienced the disharmony, the inner discord of his milieu, as a struggle between two opposing principles. In his dissolute youth, he felt the power of evil, of sin. But it was not merely an individual, personal sin: he lived "like everyone else," repeating the sins of his society, where chastity was regarded as something shameful. It was a social sin, but at the same time also the sin of his passionate, sensual paternal nature – in other words, hereditary sin. His social environment and inherited physical constitution together drove him onto the path of corruption and evil. Yet against these evil, unbridled impulses, there resisted remnants of Christian sentiment, preserved in dim childhood memories.

Already in these early impressions lay the fundamental contrast that later shaped Augustine's entire worldview: on the one hand, sin as not merely individual, but also social and hereditary; on the other, the power of good, of grace. In his On the Governance of God, Salvian said: "In almost every African I do not know what is not evil"; and elsewhere: "It is hard to find among them a good man." Combining these two sayings with all that Salvian reports about the Africans, we easily understand why, especially for an African like Augustine, the power of evil must have seemed overwhelming and unconquerable by natural human strength, while goodness, on the contrary, must have appeared something absolutely supernatural and superhuman. This explains much in Augustine's philosophy, and in particular, why, in his ethical worldview, the human element is diminished, relegated to a purely passive role, and why his system has no place for human freedom. His system is torn by the contrast between the prevailing power of evil in corrupted human nature and the irresistible power of grace, which alone can break this evil. Between these two poles, man is nothing: his freedom is wholly absorbed either from below or from above, consumed entirely in sin or in grace. In that age of universal disintegration and discord, the individual felt alone and of necessity turned inward. Thus, it is no wonder that Augustine's philosophy began with self-absorption and self-examination.

Modern literature has often pointed to his subjectivism, to his tendency toward reflection carried to the point of morbid self-listening. Protestant German historians, in particular, tend to emphasize this kindred trait in him. Central to Augustine's speculation, they tell us, is the subjective inner world of human consciousness, will, and feeling. "Everything external has for him meaning and value," says Siebeck, "only when it appears in the reflection of the inner." All objective reality interested him only in its relation to man and his inner world. What stands first for him, according to Siebeck, is the most intimate reality: the life of the human soul in God.

Augustine himself indeed writes that he wishes to know only the soul and God, and nothing more. But we would be highly unjust to our Father of the Church if we were to see in all his thought nothing but subjectivism and reduce his philosophy to mere subjective reflection. The subjectivism of that time, as already noted, corresponds to the condition of loneliness of the personality turned in upon itself. If the thinking of our Church Father had remained at mere reflection, he would never have escaped from the state of selfish isolation, intellectual and moral. He could never have risen above the individualism of his society. In any case, it was not this trait that made him the founder of medieval theocracy. In reality, he was a man of contrasts, and within his consciousness, he encompassed elements that were diverse and heterogeneous.

Having recognized the nothingness of the material, sensual world, he plunged into himself, but only in order, after perceiving the emptiness and nothingness of the self-enclosed human personality, to pass beyond that state into mystical contemplation. "Do not go outward," he says in one of his early writings, composed soon after his conversion to Christianity, "enter into yourself: truth dwells in the inner man; and if you find that your nature is changeable, then go beyond yourself as well. But remember, when you go beyond yourself, you pass beyond the soul that reasons. Strive, therefore, toward that place from which the very light of reason is kindled." Self-absorption and self-analysis, as this quotation shows, were for Augustine only the starting point of philosophy; its ultimate goal was knowledge of supernatural reality, that higher world beyond all that is subjective and human.

A strongly developed sense of self was indeed a distinctive feature of our thinker, and subjectivism was truly a trait of his character. But we must not forget that for Augustine the exclusive rule of self-feeling, the exclusive self-assertion of the individual, was the greatest evil, the principle of all evil. Throughout his life, he struggled against his subjectivism, although he never fully succeeded in overcoming it. For him, self-absorption and self-analysis were only the beginning of self-renunciation: turning inward, he found in himself only inner discord – the very struggle of the world's opposites, of good and sinful nature – from which he sought deliverance.

The path of his philosophy was from the discord and division of his personal life toward the objective world and unity. So long as we are shut within our sensual world, we find only darkness and suffering within ourselves. "Do you not see, and are you not terrified by this abyss?" Augustine exclaims. "And what is this, if not our nature – not as it once was, but as it now is. And so we seek to know it rather than truly understand it." All of Augustine's thought in his pre-Christian period was a series of giant efforts to break free from this negative, dark depth of subjective consciousness into the objective light and truth, to be freed from his sinful personality and its fatal division.

He himself says in the Confessions of that period of his life when, having already freed himself from Manichaeism, he had not yet converted to Christianity: "Trying to bring my thought into order, I sank again into the abyss, and often making efforts, I sank again and again." The only thing that lifted him toward the objective light of God, he tells us, was that his will was as sure to him as his own existence. The arguments of skeptics could never shake this inner certainty of self-consciousness. But within his very will, he found only one inner contradiction, one hopeless discord. "For this will is the cause of my sin, but I myself do not will sin, and I do what I hate. Sinning unwillingly, I would rather suffer it than do it." Thus, this condition of non-freedom is more a punishment than guilt, and a punishment that I suffer justly.

Therefore, there is something particular that rises above my contradictions: in discord itself I recognize the objective law of absolute justice – such was Augustine's reasoning. The absolute certainty of my will, of my existence, reduces to the absolute certainty of that objective good, that objective world and order, which my will demands. Division and discord are the forms of temporal reality, but peace and unity are its eternal ideal. The fundamental motive of Augustine's philosophy is the search for such a universe as would overcome the contrasts of temporal reality, its evil duality, in the unity of a universal world and rest. This search was above all a painful and tormenting process; in it, the birthpangs of a new world were joined with the death-agony of the old.

To become the progenitor of medieval thought, Augustine had to experience and overcome paganism within himself. He united and suffered within himself all the maladies of his age; in the complete sense of the word, he bore the cross of his society. Already on the path to conversion, half a Christian, Augustine recounts: "I sought, burning inwardly, whence came evil. What were the pangs of my heart in travail! What were my groans, O my God!" This was the anguish of the soul, inexpressible and incommunicable in words, which, Augustine continues, no man could share or understand, and to which God alone invisibly gave heed. Not yet fully detached from Manichaeism, he tells us further in the Confessions that he sought truth in the visible universe, outside himself, whereas the light of truth is within us. "And it is not enclosed in any place; meanwhile I looked upon things that are in definite places, and found no place in them for rest, nor did they receive me into themselves so that I could say: now it is enough, now it is well with me; nor did they permit me to return to where it would be well with me."

For a consciousness divided within itself, the whole world appears as something utterly external, alien, and hostile. Seeking something higher than himself, absolute good and truth, and questioning the external world, Augustine saw in it only what was lower, and found no peace. This alien and hostile world did not deliver him from inner unrest but instead weighed upon and oppressed his consciousness. "When I rose against God in my thoughts," he continues, "these lower beings raised themselves over me, oppressed me, giving me neither rest nor peace." The sensual world pressed upon him from without with its alien mass. When he withdrew into the depths of his consciousness, the images of material things still surrounded and pursued him, all seeming to say together: "Where are you going, so unclean and unworthy?"

No one has portrayed this inner contradiction, this deep division penetrating the inmost depths of our moral being, more profoundly and truthfully than Augustine. The absence of unity, of wholeness, is the fundamental mark of our corrupted nature. Our will prescribes one thing and does another. Therefore, it does not will with its whole being, does not prescribe with its whole being. "For it prescribes since it wills; yet what it prescribes is not done since it does not will. For will prescribes that there be will, and not another will, but itself. Therefore, it is not the whole will that prescribes, and thus what it prescribes does not exist. For if the will were whole, it would not prescribe, for what it prescribed would already be." That is, if the will were not inwardly divided, there would be no division between intention and act, and command would coincide directly with fulfillment. This abnormal state of spirit, in which our will partly wills and partly does not will, and the one personality is lost among contradictory desires and affections, Augustine calls a deformity, a sickness of the spirit. "In reality, there are two wills, since neither of them is a whole will, and what belongs to one is lacking in the other." Everything in our inner world is fragmented; everything in it is struggle, chaos, and contradiction.

Reading Augustine's Confessions, we feel an abyss of subjective consciousness opening before us, but within this abyss, we see the struggle of objective world contrasts. In it is revealed to us that psychological process which, to a greater or lesser degree, all experience who obtain faith through struggle and effort, who come to it by way of long search and doubt. At the same time, the Confessions may be regarded as a subjective reflection of the society of that age, divided between the opposite poles of unbridled sensual nature and ascetic holiness.

CHAPTER: III

Seeing division at the root of our being, Augustine interprets it as the beginning of decay and death. In our earthly life, we undergo a process of continuous dying. The conflict of spirit and flesh, this innate dualism of our nature, is for him the manifestation of death within us, and the final separation of spirit from flesh – the death of the body – is only the last earthly stage of this painful process. The first temporal manifestation of death is our natura vitiata: we perceive it in the resistance of our flesh, which does not obey the commands of consciousness, and in the inner fragmentation of our own mind and will. Death began already when the first man felt in his members "the rebellious disobedience of sensual desire"; thereby, he fell under the necessity of death. Man has no dominion over his body, and the loss of the body, physical death, is only the consistent result of the general abnormal state of our inability to subdue and control it. Death is rooted in the very nature of temporal existence, in which everything flows away without ceasing. "Man is never truly alive, insofar as he dwells in this body, which dies rather than lives"; "in this race of times we seek the present and do not find it, for it is only a passage from future to past, utterly without extension."

The evil duality lies in the very form of time: everything is split between the infinite past, which we cannot retain, and the infinite future, which, as soon as we reach it, slips into the past without filling our lives. In the midst of this restless movement, we seek and never find the present. We have nothing on which to rest, since the present does not exist; we are unceasingly dying and inwardly restless. Division, death, is the universal law of all our reality, of everything that exists in time.

The central concern of all of Augustine's philosophy revolves around this fundamental question: how to be delivered from death, how to overcome the evil duality of human nature? Before his eyes stood the ideal of the whole person, abiding in peace and rest. Thus, the fundamental question of his philosophy may also be formulated in this way: how is the human personality saved? But evil is universal and objective by nature: it lies at the foundation of both human society and the organization of the natural cosmos to which we belong as physical beings. Hence arises the further question: how is humanity saved, how is the universe saved?

The ideal whole person is conceivable only in an ideal society, in an ideal universe free from time itself, where all is one and whole, all abides in inner peace, rest, and balance. But such a universe we do not find in our experience. It is an ideal, absolutely transcendent to our earthly reality, where all is in conflict – it is the object of hope.

If the evil duality of our nature – death and sin – is the negative postulate of Augustine's philosophy, then the universe as a unity of universal peace is its positive ideal. What he sought was not only the inner good of the individual: he fully recognized that man cannot save himself by his own powers, and therefore the very question of the salvation of the person is above all a question of the objective saving principle. As sin is not merely personal or individual, but general and hereditary, so too the activity of the objective saving principle must be embodied in humanity as a whole, in the universal social order. Thus, for him, the question of the salvation of the person is at the same time social and cosmic.

Knowing this fundamental motive of Augustine's philosophical quest, we can easily understand the inner process of his development, which, through a series of stages, led him to Christianity, and we can grasp the successive genesis of his worldview. I need not enter here into the detailed biography of Augustine. The main stages of the life of this great teacher of the Church are too well known, and they interest us only insofar as they help us to understand the rise and development of his system. All of us have heard, already in school, of the stormy epoch of Augustine's youth, when, having lost his simple childhood faith and shifted from Christian foundations, he paid tribute to his time and society, living a life of petty interests of personal egoism, divided between vanity and sensuality. But even then, the external world with its pleasures did not inwardly satisfy or fulfill the future thinker. His philosophical calling, already revealed at this stage, manifested itself in him as a vague ferment, an unconscious longing for the ideal, as dissatisfaction with reality and discontent with the present. Under the influence of Cicero's Hortensius, which he read at the age of nineteen, this vague seeking turned into conscious philosophical reflection. That lost work of Cicero was an eloquent exhortation to philosophize. By Augustine's own admission, it awakened in him a conscious love of wisdom, a conscious need to seek it. "Suddenly," he says, "every vain hope became worthless to me, and with an inexpressible, fiery desire of the heart I thirsted for the immortality of wisdom." Thus, already in the earliest stage of his development, Augustine's philosophical thought bore a distinctly idealistic character. However, this youthful idealism did not manifest itself in a distinct philosophical worldview; it was merely impulsive. Philosophical reflection destroyed for him the world of illusory interests and vain dreams in which he had lived until then, and shattered his self-satisfaction. His philosophical idealism, expressed in the awareness of the discrepancy between reality and the sought-for ideal, became for him only a new source of pain and torment. It did not heal him; on the contrary, it deepened the painful state of moral division and discord. Hence arose that pessimistic disposition which soon found expression in Augustine's Manichaeism.

Turning from the dark depths of subjective consciousness to contemplation of the objective universe, he nevertheless could not rise to a purely epic relation to it; instead, he carried over his own inner contradictions into the objective cosmos. The inner struggle he discovered within himself was hypostatized for him as the struggle between two objective world principles, the opposition of two hostile substances: good and evil. Looking carefully at Manichaeism, we see that this religious-philosophical system – especially in the Western form Augustine received – is nothing other than a peculiar pessimism of the age. It was, above all, in Professor Harnack's words, "a consistent, sharp dualism in the form of a fantastic speculation about nature." The whole world, according to the Manicheans, was the result of a chance union of good and evil principles, of light and darkness, conceived materialistically as two substantial entities, as physical light and darkness. When the prince of darkness, Satan, burst into the kingdom of light, he captured part of the light-substance. The origin of all existence – heaven with its stars, the earth, and all living beings – was conditioned by this captivity of particles of the good light-substance, which strive to be freed from the bonds of the evil principle, Satan, who enslaved them, and to return to the kingdom of light from which they were violently torn. In this liberation lies the ultimate goal of the creative process, the ultimate aim of the universe's development.

Thus, in the Manichean system, evil is essentially active, while good is passive; its role is reduced to mere self-preservation and self-defense against the advancing power of evil. Good can and must in the end be entirely freed from evil; light must be separated from darkness. But evil is indestructible; it is as eternal as good, and the realm of light cannot wholly overcome it or turn it into itself. The ethical disposition corresponding to this dualistic system is pessimism – the consistent result of a doctrine which places division, irreconcilable and eternal enmity, at the foundation of all that exists. The world, as a dual offspring of good and evil, is contradictory, false, and destined for abolition.

The practical task of man in the cosmos is to destroy this abnormal union by means of ascetic struggle. In man, the struggle of the world principles reaches its highest tension – for he is a dual being: created by Satan in his image and likeness, yet containing in himself light-particles to a far greater degree than other creatures. Satan concentrated in him the captive particles of good in order through him to rule over them; thus, in him, both hostile elements reach their highest earthly concentration. By giving himself over to carnal passions and selfish self-assertion, man maintains the captivity of the light-particles; through eating and natural procreation, he serves the ends of the evil principle, binding good to the kingdom of darkness with new chains and passing on the union from generation to generation. By contrast, through ascetic self-mortification and self-denial, through fasting and continence, he can and must aid in the liberation of the captive particles of light. Yet man can accomplish this highest practical task only insofar as he is enlightened by knowledge.

The task of knowledge, of gnosis, is to make clear to mankind the fundamental abnormality of existence, the basic contradiction of the universe, and thereby to prepare the act of self-denial, the self-annihilation of the cosmos through the ascetic struggle of man.

What, then, drew Augustine to Manichaeism? First, the rationalist character of the system, which did not rest on external authority but appealed to human reason, attempted to give a rational explanation of existence. This rationalism appealed to the thinker who, by his own admission, was at that time both repelled and enticed by the simplicity of the Gospel; he sought a scientific worldview. Second, the sensuous and fantastic character of this doctrine, in which Gnostic rationalism coexisted with unrestrained Eastern imagination, was very congenial to his southern African temperament. Finally, third, as noted above, it is hypothesized that ethical and psychological dualism, which Augustine discovered in himself through deep self-analysis. "Loving unity in virtue," he says, "and hating discord in vice, I observed unity in the one case, and in the other a certain division. It seemed to me that in this unity consisted the rational soul, and in it the nature of truth and the supreme good was contained. But at the foundation of the division of irrational life, I knew not what substance and nature of the supreme evil, which is not only a substance but has true life," and, moreover, a substance not created by God but coeternal with Him. He conceived the good as a sexless thinking substance, calling it the Monad, and evil as the Dyad.

This Manichean period of Blessed Augustine is a phenomenon closely analogous to the pessimism of our own time. The modern pessimist Schopenhauer, like Augustine, projects his subjective contradictions into the contemplation of the objective cosmos, hypostatizing the inner division of his personality. He, too, places an evil duality at the foundation of all existence: the world, in his view, is likewise the contradictory creation of two hostile principles – mad, evil will, the principle of strife and discord, and will-less intellect, whose entire task is reduced to passive resistance against the evil will, to freeing itself from it. The very path of liberation in Schopenhauer is the same as in Mani; for in both the world-crisis is accomplished in man, who, being the most perfect objectification of the satanic principle of will, is at the same time the highest representative and bearer of world-intellect. The task of man in Schopenhauer's system also consists in recognizing the nothingness and evil nature of existence and in freeing the world from its contradictions through ascetic self-denial. In Schopenhauer, as in Augustine, we observe the exact coincidence of results between subjective reflection – the work of a Western thinker – and the sensuous, fantastic worldview of Eastern religions, the same gravitation toward the religious acosmism of the East. For if the Buddhist Schopenhauer abolishes the one cosmos in nirvana, while at the same time splitting it in the dualism of world-essence and maya, so too Augustine loses the unity of the cosmos, acknowledging two Manichean substances and seeing in the universe the result of contradiction. In Schopenhauer, as in Augustine, Western subjectivism, in its extreme and one-sided development, touches upon the spontaneous objectivism of the East.

This coincidence appears to us comprehensible and by no means accidental: extreme subjectivism and extreme objectivism resemble one another in a typical result – namely, that both lose the conditional boundary between subjective and objective, inner and outer. Whether we interpret all that is inward as a phenomenon of objective substance, or, conversely, all that is outward as a reflection of the inner, in both cases, the result is the same: the fusion of subjective and objective. Our inner sphere passes into the objective world and is materialized in it; or else, conversely, our inner states are hypostatized into objective substance, and all that is external is understood in their image and likeness. The results coincide – this is the secret of all Eastern influences upon Western philosophy.

Augustine's disposition in this Manichean period was one of gloomy, profound despair. He later saw the reason for this in the precariousness of his then views of God. The Manichean deity is consubstantial with us by nature; our soul is a particle of this deity, and therefore it does not exalt us above ourselves, above the weakness and frailty of our nature, nor does it deliver us from our sufferings. On the contrary, it shares our indigence and imbecility. If our soul is a part of the deity, then God, along with us, "is perverted by our folly, is changed in our fall, and, losing His perfection, suffers violence and needs help, is crushed by misfortune, and shamed by bondage." From such a god, we cannot expect salvation: it is instead in need of our aid for its own deliverance, and thus the Manichean worldview appears cheerless and hopeless. Augustine felt this with particular clarity when, grieving over the death of a friend, he sought and did not find consolation in Manichean doctrine. He himself aptly characterizes his mood at that time as taedium vivendi et moriendi metus – weariness of living and fear of dying; in him, the sense of the emptiness of the present was heightened by hopelessness about the future. "All that exists grew loathsome to me," he says, "the very light itself was loathsome, all was loathsome except groaning and tears." And again: "When I tried to rest my soul in the false god, the creation of my imagination, it fell again into emptiness and collapsed upon me anew; and I remained in myself, in that unhappy place where it was intolerable for me to be, yet whence I could not escape. For where could my heart flee from my heart? Where could I go without myself following?" Seeking salvation in Manichaeism, he found in it only a reflection of his subjective contradictions.

In a world where all is illusory and false, there is nothing objectively certain, nothing true. Even our own consciousness is contradictory. If all in the world, including ourselves, is falsehood and contradiction, if there is no truth self-contained, then no objective knowledge is possible. From dualistic pessimism, it is but one step to skeptical despair. And thus, disappointed in Manichaeism, Augustine fell into the skepticism of the New Academy. However, this skepticism was only a fleeting moment in his development, and he never fully mastered his energetic and passionate nature.

It was only a temporary and brief state of hesitation and indecision. "It seemed to me," Augustine writes, "that those philosophers who are called Academics were more cautious than others, in affirming that one must doubt everything and remain in suspense about all things; and I resolved to leave the Manichees, thinking I ought not remain in a sect which I already preferred less than some philosophers."

It is clear that here we are not dealing with absolute skepticism, nor with any fixed and definite worldview, but only with recognition of the relative rightness of the skeptical philosophers. They are right in this, that they oppose arbitrary dogmatic assumptions with a doubt in the powers and capacities of human reason. They are more right than others insofar as they are more humble than others. But if man is unable to know truth by his own powers, it does not follow from this that truth itself does not exist. If man, left to himself, cannot master truth, then truth may meet his efforts and reveal itself to him. Inaccessible to rational knowledge, it may be the object of revelation. In that case, skepticism itself becomes an act of humility, a passive submission of human reason to action from above.

Augustine's skepticism was indeed for him only a transitional stage to the mystical worldview of the Neoplatonic philosophers. "Thou didst stir me, O God," we read in the Confessions, "by inward incentives, so that I burned with impatience until I came to a certain inward vision of Thee." The torment of doubt and hesitation was only the expression of unsatisfied seeking, and Augustine's skepticism was only the consequence of his inborn mysticism, which would not allow him to rest in dogmatic constructions. We have already seen how the inner certainty of self-consciousness lifted him above skeptical doubt: let all that exists be uncertain, yet I am and I will. In the very division of my consciousness and will, I find unity, as an absolute demand, as an ideal. This unity is found neither in external reality, accessible to sense experience, nor in myself; it rises above everything I find in my experience. It is an ideal immeasurably surpassing all earthly things, absolutely transcendent. I come to it only by abstraction from everything external, by inward contemplation. Only a consciousness collected within itself, inwardly concentrated and detached from all that is sensuous, can come to recognition of this unity beyond our consciousness itself. The certainty of my self-consciousness, of my will, is at the same time the absolute certainty of its transcendent ideal.

It was precisely to this result that Augustine was led under the influence of reading the Neoplatonic philosophers, as is evident from his own account. Urged by them to enter into himself, he continues, "I entered into the innermost depths of my being, guided by Thee, O God, and could do so because Thou wast my helper. I entered, and I saw with the eye of the soul, above that same eye of my soul, above my mind, the immutable light

– not this ordinary light, visible to all flesh. It was above my mind, not like oil upon water or heaven above earth, but it was superior, because it made me, and I was inferior, because I was made by it. He who knows truth knows that light, and he who knows that light knows eternity. Love knows it. O eternal truth, true love, beloved eternity! Thou art my God, for Thee do I sigh day and night."

This was no longer the sensuous Manichean deity spread through space, but an absolutely supersensuous principle. This objective, immaterial light, shining within us, is the perfect contrast with our meager, feeble consciousness. "Thou didst smite my feeble gaze," Augustine continues, "with Thy mighty rays, and I trembled with love and awe, and I saw that I was far from Thee, dwelling in a land unlike Thee. And it was as if I heard Thy voice from on high: 'I am the food of the strong; grow, and thou shalt feed on Me. But thou shalt not change Me into thyself, as thou changest thy bodily food, but thou shalt be changed into Me.'"

If truth is not diffused in the external world, nor contained in space, whether finite or infinite, does it follow from this that truth itself does not exist? To this question of my consciousness, says Augustine, I heard Thy voice in answer, as if from afar: I am He who is.

In this Divine "I", Augustine at last finds the object of his search. In the energy of God's personal self-consciousness, the lost unity is restored and the single person is saved. Here is the objective place where the human "I" finds its rest, the inner peace that delivers from the torment of divided consciousness. Having lost God, we wander without finding a place for ourselves, and only in Him do we recover ourselves, come back to ourselves. "Where was I, O Lord, when I sought Thee? Thou wast before me, but I had gone out from myself; I could not find myself, and still less Thee." God is "the life of my life." Without Him, we lose the integrity of our being and are deprived of inner peace. "Thou hast made us for Thee, O Lord," we read in the Confessions, "and our heart is restless until it rests in Thee." Having found God, we awaken as from a heavy sleep. "I awoke in Thee, and otherwise I saw in Thee the infinite, and this sight was not of the flesh. And I looked upon all that exists and saw that all things owe their being to Thee, and in Thee all finite things abide – but not as in some extended place, for Thou holdest all within Thyself by the power of truth."

Thus, Augustine assimilated Neoplatonic elements; yet, during this period, he was not wholly a Neoplatonist. For him, the practical, vital task stands foremost, and the speculative, mystical ideal of those philosophers did not satisfy him by reason of its abstractness.

The transcendent "One" of the Neoplatonists does not overcome the division of earthly reality; their contemplative mysticism coexists with a profound dualism. Neoplatonism is torn by the contrast between the abstract divine unity – transcendent, supersensuous, and absolutely unincarnate – and matter, which is hostile and alien to divine reality. This matter, the principle of all imperfection and evil in the world, resists God. He does not create it; it exists equally eternally and cannot be inwardly transformed or destroyed by Him. Between heaven and earth, between the Divine and the material, lies irreconcilable enmity; discord of contending principles, strife, and division form the basis of all that exists. Clearly, such a system could not overcome Manichean pessimism, and Augustine had not abandoned Eastern dualism only to fall into Greek dualism.

We have seen that the longing to be delivered from this fatal dualism is the vital nerve of his philosophy. Philosophy, as I have said, is for him at the same time a practical, religious task – the task of salvation. The divine world is for him above all the objective, saving principle. Meanwhile, the Neoplatonic "One" is abstract; all that is individual and personal in it is denied; the human person can come to its contemplation only through self-annihilation in an ecstatic state. In this impersonal divine cosmos, the individual finds no place, no peace. The impersonal Deity is indifferent and alien to man; it does not guard him, it does not save him.

The object of Augustine's search is God, concerned with man's salvation, in whom the human, the personal, is not destroyed but preserved, receiving higher content and center. Hence, Neoplatonism in his hands immediately assumes a distinctly Christian hue. In place of Plotinus' and Porphyry's abstract "One," there stands for him the energy of God's personal self-consciousness, which enters into dialogue with man, answering his quest. To free us from the division of our earthly reality, to save us from suffering and death, divine unity must become fact within our reality by penetrating it with itself. To save man, God must enter into an immediate, intimate relation with him, face to face – in a word, must become incarnate. To save humanity as a race, as a society, the divine order must be embodied in a universal social organization. Such is the logical process that drives Augustine from Neoplatonism to Christianity and the Church.

What repels him in the Neoplatonists is precisely the absence of humanity in their conception of the Deity. He adopts entirely their doctrine of the eternal Divine Logos, paraphrasing it in the familiar words of John's Gospel. But these profound speculations of the Neoplatonists, seemingly so consonant with Christian doctrine, do not satisfy the future Father of the Church, because they lack the idea of the Incarnation, the God-Manhood, which alone can overcome dualism and reconcile the human, the earthly, with the divine. Their deity does not stoop to human weakness, does not come to the aid of the suffering, nor by forgiveness lift from us the burden of sin.

Alongside Neoplatonism, Augustine was influenced by another powerful force that irresistibly drew him in the same direction. At the very moment when the mystical ideal was becoming for him a practical imperative, when he sought divine unity in earthly, concrete embodiment, he encountered the mighty figure of Ambrose. There is no need here for a detailed portrait of this great hierarch. It is enough to note those features of his character that influenced the worldview of his brilliant disciple. Ambrose may be called the concrete embodiment of the powerful ecclesiastical organization.

In him, the Christian idea appears as a crushing, irresistible force, the vivid image of that omnipotent grace which triumphs over human evil in its most powerful manifestations, sustaining the struggle against supreme human power. In

Ambrose, the representative of the religious idea triumphs over human might at its highest level. He emerged victorious in his conflicts with the Arian empress, and he humbled to the dust so colossal a figure as Theodosius the Great. At the same time, he personified the contrast between the weakness and insignificance of secular authority in the feeble emperors, such as Gratian and Valentinian II, and the grandeur of spiritual authority in the representative of the Church. This bishop, who asserted that the state is in the Church and not the Church in the state, that the Church is prior and greater than the state, truly ruled and triumphed over temporal power, appearing at times as stern judge and teacher, at times as guardian and tutor of half-witted emperors. By his character and tendencies, he was in many respects the forerunner of the great medieval popes, the precursor of the Gregories and Innocents.

Augustine sought the religious idea in concrete historical embodiment. And here the Christian idea appeared to him in the energy of comprehensive practical activity. He sought the objective saving principle, the divine unity, as the objective norm of human life and activity, and he encountered the mighty universal organization of the Church represented in the colossal person of the great bishop. But Ambrose impressed him not only by the external authority of his greatness and power. He reconciled ecclesiastical authority with scholarly culture; his word sounded not only as external command but also carried inner persuasive force. He embodied the Church not only as an external unity, but as a rational order, as an organic, inner unity. Listening to Ambrose, Augustine was for the first time convinced of the possibility of rational interpretation of Christian doctrine, assured of the absence of any fundamental contradiction between rational knowledge and objective revelation. In Ambrose, the Christian ideal appeared to Augustine as the all-embracing rule of the divine order over life, as the omnipotent Church ruling over individual and society, as a theocracy in which the secular principle is absorbed by the spiritual. The impression of Ambrose's personality, as has been said, left an indelible mark on Augustine's worldview. His Christian ideal was bound forever with that impression, and remained forever a theocratic ideal. To this, the deep kinship of character between the two saints also contributed.

As noted above, the central impression of Augustine's entire life is the contrast of sin and omnipotent grace. If grace is all-powerful, and man's will is nothing, then it follows that for salvation, man must wholly sacrifice his freedom, surrendering himself entirely to objective grace. The individual must disappear in the objective order of grace; man receives his significance and meaning only as an organ of universal divine rule. To omnipotent grace corresponds the all-ruling Church as its embodiment. Thus, the influence of Ambrose coincided with the central motive of our Father's entire life and worldview.

I need not recount here the too well-known details of his conversion to Christianity. What interests us is the inner history of his worldview, not the outward events of his life. It is enough to note one characteristic feature of this conversion. Augustine himself ascribes that profound inner transformation in him to an inward miracle. At the moment when his sufferings, the torments of unsatisfied seeking, reached their extreme limit, an outward impulse delivered him from doubt and hesitation. He heard a voice saying tolle et lege ("take and read"), and heard it with bodily ears, yet he attributed it to a revelation from above; and opening, at the prompting of that voice, the Holy Scripture, he found in it a text answering his quest, applied it to himself, and thus his conversion was accomplished.

For Augustine, it is deeply characteristic that even in his conversion, he sees as it were the violence of grace over weak human nature. Grace appears here already as an irresistible power, acting upon man from within and from without, not only through inner impulses but also through outward shocks. It leads us to objective unity not only through the inward illumination of our mind and heart but also through external compulsion.

The account in the Confessions was written about fourteen years after Augustine's conversion, from the standpoint of a fully formed doctrine of grace. And we may agree with Gaston Boissier and Harnack that at this time, Augustine was inclined to represent his conversion as more sudden than it really was. In fact, it was not sudden, but on the contrary, prepared by the whole preceding development of his life. Looking back from a distance, he could see his past in a new light and might misjudge the meaning of particular events, but no one could suspect him of inventing the events themselves.

What remains for us, then, is the significant fact that Augustine's conversion was linked for him with the impression of an external miracle. Already in this impression lay the germ of the fatalistic theory of grace that he later developed, according to which grace acts upon our will not only as an inner necessity but also as an external fate, and our will becomes the automatic organ of its decrees.

We have followed the formation of Blessed Augustine's worldview to the point where it became fixed, firmly established on a Christian foundation. Looking closely at the doctrine he built on this foundation, we see that his past did not vanish without a trace; the elements that shaped Augustine the pagan continued to live in his Christian consciousness. This pagan past gives us the key to understanding the religious-philosophical system of the great teacher of the Church. Augustine's development, as we have seen, completed a full circle, returning after long wandering to its starting point – to the Christian worldview of his mother.

Looking deeper into this worldview, we see that it preserved the influential philosophical idealism that awoke in him under the influence of Cicero's Hortensius. We also find Manichean elements in it. He opposed Manichean pessimism with an optimistic theodicy, while retaining the element of truth within it: for while an optimist in hope of a better life, he maintained, in full accord with Christianity, a pessimistic attitude toward earthly life. But while preserving that element of truth found in Manichaeism, he did not wholly free himself from its falsehood. Entering the fray immediately after his conversion, Augustine defended against Manichean dualism the unity of the divine order of the universe. Against the dualism of Mani's followers, he developed a strictly monotheistic doctrine; against their rationalistic subjectivism, he opposed the objective authority of the Church. Seeking salvation from the divided universe, he developed the doctrine of the ideal unity of the world-plan eternally contained in the divine consciousness. To the divided human consciousness, he opposed objective revelation. Yet even in the struggle, he did not wholly free himself from the influence of his opponents, and unconscious Manichaeism continued to manifest itself in his worldview.

In Augustine's teaching, evil no longer limits God from without, but is included within the world plan as a necessary moment of divine predestination, logically flowing from God's self-revelation about creation. Evil ceases to be an external boundary for God, but becomes instead an inner necessity of the divine will: it is a necessary moment in the self-disclosure of the divine idea, like the dark background upon which the beauty and goodness of God's thought of creation are revealed. Evil – created egoism – is not overcome inwardly, in potency, but is forced into the world-plan as a necessary means to a goal alien to it, the good. Augustine could never entirely overcome Manichean dualism, and the unity he opposed to it was a forced, external unity.

Looking further into our Father's worldview, we find in it that skepticism which, as we have seen, is expressed in the humility of the mind, in the recognition of man's inability by his own powers alone to know truth. Needless to say, it retains the mystical ideal of the Neoplatonists; like them, it regards all that exists sub specie aeterni, relating all particular things to their eternal, supersensuous idea. Then, as we noted earlier, it bears the stamp of Ambrose's powerful influence. These elements of Blessed Augustine's worldview are partly essential moments of Christian consciousness and partly adulterated with falsehood, characterizing the one-sided form of Christianity that found expression in his writings.

All who do not receive Christianity as a gift, who do not inherit it, but come to it through reason and will by way of free inquiry, inevitably pass through the idealist impulses of youth and the despair of pessimists and skeptics: to believe in the mystical ideal of Christianity one must, with the pessimists, despair of earthly reality; but to submit to the Church, one must, with the skeptics, renounce rationalist conceit and the pride of reason. To be a Christian, one must believe in the supernatural idea and acknowledge divine authority over oneself.

The stages of Augustine's development are thus in some measure necessary stages within Christianity itself, and his Confessions may rightly be called a phenomenology of Christian consciousness. But the worldview of our Father, as already noted and as we shall yet see, contains much that is subjective and local falsehood. We have said that he never fully overcame Manichean dualism within himself, and that the unity he opposed to the followers of Mani was a forced, external unity. This fact had incalculable consequences not only for Augustine himself but for the entire Western form of Christianity of which he was the forefather and founder.

The age of Augustine, as noted at the beginning of this chapter, was marked by the clash and conflict of two opposite poles – the Church with its unity and the atomized, isolated individual. What, then, could Western, Latin Christianity oppose to the striving of the free personality and the anarchic individualism of the two societies? We see this in Augustine's system. To individual freedom, he opposed the compulsion of grace; to disorder and anarchy, the unity of the divine plan as an external order embracing all that exists, which does not abolish evil and egoism but subordinates them to its ends. The divine unity, as universal law of all that is, and as the ideal norm of all that ought to be, as the productive cause and final goal of all that exists – such is Augustine's fundamental thought, carried consistently through his whole system. But it is not a free unity, in which free God enters into covenant with free creature; it is an abstract unity, in which God rules the world only from without, a compelled, violent unity.

Prophet and forerunner of medieval Catholicism, Augustine already contained within himself both its positive and its opposing sides. At the moment of his conversion, all the elements of his Christian worldview were already present, and all the rest was only the development and application of those principles which had ripened in his consciousness by that time.

Surveying his entire literary activity, we may distinguish three stages in the development of his teaching, corresponding to his struggle with three Christian heresies: Manichaeism, Donatism, and Pelagianism.

1. Against the Manichees, he developed the doctrine of the objective unity of the world-plan and opposed their rationalism with the unity of Church authority.

2. Against the Donatists, the same principle of world-order unity was specified as unitas ecclesiae; to their ecclesiastical particularism, he opposed Catholic universalism.

3. Against the Pelagians, who denied grace, he asserted the unity of the action of grace as the objective saving principle, unity as universal predestination triumphing over individual human freedom.

In all three stages, the same principle – ideal unity – was specified as the architectonic principle of the universe, as the principle of the social organization of society, and as the content of subjective human freedom. Developing particular sides of his doctrine against heresies that denied one or another side of Christianity, Augustine concentrated and summed it up in all its fullness against the pagans. Here, the ideal of our thinker received its most complete and perfect expression, formulated as the Civitas Dei, as the unity of universal divine rule.

PART: II

Augustine – Apologist of the Theocratic Ideal of Western Christianity

CHAPTER: I

Three significant historical events mark the chronological boundaries of Blessed Augustine's literary activity. His work begins under Theodosius the Great, at the moment of the last political unification of both halves of the Roman Empire and on the eve of its final disintegration; it reaches its apogee at the sack of Rome by the Goths under Alaric; and it ends with the conquest of Africa by the Vandals, which began shortly before Augustine's death. This coincidence of the beginning, the peak, and the end of the great Father's activity with three world-historical events is not the result of mere historical accident. For Augustine's worldview, it is no accident that at the very beginning of his apologetic work, the Roman Empire, unified under Theodosius, begins to fall apart. That event immediately raised the question: How can Roman cultural unity be preserved despite the collapse of the state? From that moment, Roman unity ceased to be purely political, but it continued to exist as an ecclesiastical unity; unitas Romana survived only as unitas ecclesiae, unitas catholica. Hence follows the conclusion that a disintegrating society can save its unity only in the universal unity of the Church, which alone binds East and West together; that, at least in relation to that society, this universal unity is the supreme saving principle.

Thus, partly in response to historical events, and more often anticipating them, began the activity of the greatest of the apologists for Christian unity. It is likewise significant that the culmination of his apologetic creativity coincided with the sack of Rome by Alaric; for the destruction of Rome was a powerful summons to build something new.

The capture of Rome dealt a mortal blow to the Roman pagan ideal embodied in the cult of imperial omnipotence. The victory of the Goths overthrew not only Roman power but also the Roman pagan deity. But while it destroyed pagan Rome, this victory bore eloquent witness to the vitality and mission of the Christian Church. While they gave Rome over to fire and sword, Alaric's warriors halted reverently before Christian sanctuaries, and the defeated found salvation and refuge in them from the rage of the conquerors. The Church alone stood firm amidst the general collapse, transforming Rome's defeat into her own greatest triumph; she alone, with her temples spared from the flames, represented Rome as the eternal city. With the fall of Rome, the old question arose again with renewed urgency: how to save a disintegrating society?

In response to the fall of the ancient capital, Augustine conceived his most excellent work, in which the Roman political idea of the city of the world is opposed by the Christian idea of the universal City of God, and in which Christian theocracy is solemnly proclaimed as the one true, eternal, and not-made-by-hands city. On the smoking ruins of pagan, Caesarean Rome, Augustine laid the ideal foundation of Christian, Catholic Rome.

It is also significant that Augustine's death coincided with the beginning of the Vandal conquest of Africa. By severing Africa, Rome's source of grain, this conquest deprived the city of the material conditions of its existence, condemned it to famine, and was almost equivalent to its annihilation. Yet once again, this turned into the Church's greatest triumph: the Church, as at the sack of Rome, alone emerged unscathed from the flames. The victory that struck down the state gave new strength to the Church, which now in North Africa remained the sole representative of Roman culture against the barbarian Germanic world. The invasion of the Arian barbarians compelled the Roman population to rally around the Catholic Church, and, paradoxically, the Vandal victory furthered Augustine's own work by striking a mortal blow at the Donatist schism, which until then had torn most of the African population away from the universal Church. This schism – above all, a reaction of local African nationalism against Roman institutions and against the universal Church – lost its ground after the conquest of Africa, and its meaning and significance evaporated. Under the Vandals, Catholicism ceased to be the ruling Church, and thus it could attract its former opponents, the Donatists. For Donatists, the true Church was above all the persecuted, martyr Church; under the rule of barbarians hostile to all non-Arians alike, they drew close to their former enemies, the Catholics, in shared suffering. The Donatist schism all but disappeared, and on the ruins of political unity, ecclesiastical unity was restored. The City of God grew stronger as it came into contact with the barbarian world, and the apologist of ecclesiastical unity died at the threshold of this new Germanic age, as if bequeathing to it his work to continue and complete.

The questions around which the great apologist's thought revolved, and his answers, were suggested by the significant historical events of his age. Upon examining his apologetic activity closely, we see that it is essentially the proclamation of divine rule as the universal law of the universe and the guiding principle of world social organization. The gradual destruction of old Rome and the building of the new – that is, the chief historical task of the age – defines the historical frame of this preaching. The ideal of the universal, eternal city, built not on the frail human foundation doomed to ruin, but on the eternal divine foundation – the ideal of the City of God – is its beginning, middle, and end. To be convinced of this, let us try to embrace Augustine's apologetic activity as a whole.

What, one might ask, could there be in common among the diverse opponents with whom Augustine had to struggle in defense of the Christian idea? What unites such diverse heresies and sects – Manichaeans, Donatists, and Pelagians? And what do these Christian heresies have in common with Roman paganism, against which Augustine's Civitas Dei was directed? Apparently, just as there was no solidarity or unity among Augustine's opponents, so there seems to be no central interest, no guiding idea, giving unity to his apologetic work.

Indeed, this conclusion is reached by the

greater part of German Protestant scholars, especially Reuter and, after him, Harnack. "Of a system of Augustine, there can be no question," says the latter. "Reuter's chief merit is to have proved the impossibility of constructing Augustine's system and of eliminating the contradictions it contains." According to these scholars, against his various opponents, the great apologist was guided each time by different interests, changing his standpoint; moreover, as an apologist of ecclesiastical practice, he was often obliged to defend the existing customs and principles of the Church even when they conflicted with his own personal religious disposition. Hence, there are many contradictions in his teaching, the lack of wholeness and unity. For example, his doctrine of free will, developed in response to the Pelagians, contradicts what he taught on the same subject against the Manicheans. His anti-Pelagian doctrine of grace contradicts his doctrine of the Church, which he developed in response to the Donatists.

We must acknowledge, along with the named German historians, that Augustine indeed contains a notable number of contradictions. We not only do not intend to gloss over them, but will make the reader acquainted with them. It is equally valid to argue that Augustine's teaching cannot be presented or studied as a philosophical system, although it contains a strong philosophical element. There is always a significant difference between the philosopher and the apologist: the philosopher builds their own system, while the apologist defends a worldview that exists and develops independently of them, historically formed before them, and given to them from without. Therefore, the unity of a system, the unity of doctrine in an apologist, depends first on whether there is such unity in the material with which he deals, and second, on whether a single interest guides him, a single idea, in his relation to that material. Suppose the presence of such a guiding interest can be shown. In that case, the doctrine under discussion must be recognized as a system, despite subjective contradictions – even if the apologist's personal disposition often fails to harmonize with the principle he defends.

Regarding Augustine, upon examining his teachings, we indeed encounter numerous inconsistencies. But since there is no human teaching, neither religious nor philosophical, which is perfectly logical and free of contradiction – since a wholly logical system is but an unattainable ideal of human reason – it is not valid to deny any doctrine the name of system merely because it contains contradictions. In that case, there would be no system at all deserving of the name. In general, we recognize as a system any doctrine pervaded by a single ideal or principle, and not one that is merely a mechanical combination of heterogeneous principles externally bound together. To deny a doctrine the significance of a system, it is not enough to show its contradictions; it is necessary also to show that these contradictions are the result of the clash of opposite elements not bound together in that doctrine by any common ideal or interest; that therefore the doctrine is not an organic unity, but only a mechanical combination.

As for Augustine's teaching, if it seems to some German scholars a heap of contradictions united only by the personality of its author, the fault lies not with Augustine but with themselves. The fault lies chiefly in the dogmatic interest that leads them to look at historical events and doctrines through the prism of their own confession. Many of Augustine's teachings – for example, his doctrine of grace, in which he appears in some sense as a forerunner of Luther – are acknowledged by them as evangelical and praised. Other of his teachings – for example, his doctrine of the Church, in which he appears as a forerunner of Catholicism – they regard with extreme hostility, as "vulgar-Catholic" elements. Thus, they miss the close organic connection that binds together the teaching of the great Father, and arbitrarily and artificially divide it into evangelical and non-evangelical elements. In particular, some scholars, like Reuter, are unable to grasp the unity of Augustine's ideal because of their very method of research – conscientious and thorough, but too petty and, so to speak, microscopic.

Examining any doctrine through a magnifying glass, we always risk losing ourselves in the details; exaggerating the significance of particular contradictions, we will never be able to see the unity of the whole. This is especially true of something so vast and grand as Augustine's teaching. To grasp its unity, to embrace it with a single view, one must step back from it and strive to see it as a link in the universal historical process. Only then will our eyes cease to be dazzled by the multitude of heterogeneous elements that make it up, and we shall discern within it the unity of thought and plan.

CHAPTER: II

For all their diversity, the opponents of Blessed Augustine stand upon common historical ground and converge, if not in what they affirm, then at least in what they deny. All of them, in one form or another, rise against the ideal of a single divine organization of the universe and of human society. All are, in one way or another, enemies of the Christian theocratic ideal, though they attack it from different sides.

From the standpoint of Manichaean teaching, as noted earlier, the world is not the creation of a single principle but of two gods. The world is not a single temple of the one God, not a unified kingdom of His, but the product of two hostile realms. At the foundation of the universe, there is no single architectural principle, no unified order. In the world, not only God but also Satan reigns eternally. The task of the Christian apologist in response to the Manicheans is to demonstrate the unity of the universe's organization, the unity of the cosmic order, and to present the world as a single whole under the power of one God. Against the doctrine that divides the world between two kingdoms, it must be shown that the one God reigns eternally. The architectural unity of the universe, the world as the realization of a single eternal plan, divine rule as a fact of eternal reality – such is the central theme of Augustine's anti-Manichaean works. Closely tied to this is the doctrine of church authority, developed in those same writings. The truth of church authority is demonstrated by the universal spread of the Church, which represents the consensus of peoples (consensus gentium). For Augustine, the Church has authority as the representative of the one divine order, divine power extending over the entire universe.

If Manichaeism denies the unity of cosmic organization, the Donatist schism is a direct attack upon the unity of the universal Church, which in the social order embodies divine unity. For Donatists, the earthly Church is not a universal edifice but a society of saints, the elect. The saving power of the Church and her sacraments rests not in her objective gifts of grace but in the subjective virtue of the ministers who administer them. Therefore, a sacrament performed by an unworthy person, convicted of manifest sins, is, from the Donatist perspective, invalid and undeserving of the name. The saving power of the Church is conditioned by the personal virtue of its hierarchy; the defining mark of the true Church is thus not its objective universal organization, but the personal holiness of its leaders. This personal holiness – or rather, the absence of manifest vices – constitutes for Donatists the purity and sanctity of the Church spoken of by the Apostle (Eph. 5:27), who calls it "the Church without spot or wrinkle." The universal Church, in its teaching, disgraced itself after the Diocletian persecution by not only retaining in its ranks bishops who had, under fear, denied the faith and handed over the Scriptures to pagans, but also leaving them in their office. From that moment, the Church ceased to be the spotless bride of Christ and became a society of traitors. Its sacraments ceased to be sacraments, and its unity lost saving power. Most telling of all, the true Church for the Donatists – the Church of saints and martyrs – was confined within the territorial bounds of their African community, in opposition to the "overseas Church," as they contemptuously called the universal Church. Thus, their doctrine expresses not merely the pride of individual bishops but above all the national arrogance of the Donatist African community.

By a tendentious interpretation of Scripture, the Donatists tried to prove that all prophecies about the Church referred to Africa, that the Africans were the chosen people, bearers of God. Hence, the African, i.e., Donatist, Church was the Church as it ought to be. For them, the churchly ideal coincided with reality, and the visible earthly Church (their African community) appeared as its perfect embodiment. In fact, behind these dogmatic formulas lay the protest of Punic nationalism against a Church not tied to any one people, against the universal Church. The Donatist denial was directed precisely against the principle of the Church's universal organization, which transcends all visible manifestations and does not coincide with the Church in her temporal, earthly condition.

Naturally, given the close bond and special relation between Church and state in the Western Empire, the Donatist schism was as anti-political as it was anti-ecclesiastical. It is clear that Western emperors, seeking salvation from their own weakness in the Church, allied themselves with the Church, which stood on a firmer foundation. Unable to build and support the state on the fragile virtue of Donatist clergy, they preferred to rely on the solid foundation of universal organization embodied in the Catholic Church. Steeped in the tradition of universal political unity, the Empire could not side with a local nationalist movement; by natural affinity, it had to align itself with the Church that represented universal social unity – the universal Church. This is why the Donatist schism opposed equally both the Catholic Church, as the Roman state Church, and the Empire, as a Catholic polity. Donatism expressed the revolt of African nationalism against the Roman concept of universal unity; hence, all discontented elements of North African society rallied under its banner against the Roman Church and its rule. The movement of the circumcellions joined them – a popular rural uprising predating Donatism, rooted in agrarian protest against the Roman land system that enslaved peasants as serfs or tenants of a few large landowners. At the first appearance of the Donatists, the circumcellions allied with them in shared hatred of Roman institutions. Thus, a movement older than Donatism, born of agrarian grievances, continued in alliance with it under the form of Christian schism. In general, we see the Donatists at the head of all African separatist movements: allied with Firmus, the Moorish king, with the rebel prince and African general Gildo, and finally, at their call, with the Vandals whose invasion proved their Nemesis.

Between the Donatists and the Church raged the same fatal dispute that troubled the entire Roman West: the question of the ideal social organization, one that saved both society and the individual. This question was especially urgent at that time, when, amid the rising tide of barbarian invasions, the existence of both society and person hung by a thread, threatened at every moment.

Given these features of the Donatist movement, the apologist's task was:

1. To defend the principle of the Church's unity and her universal organization, existing objectively and salvifically independently of the personal holiness of the clergy.

2. To point out the distinction between the Church in her visible, earthly reality and in her eternal ideal. In view of the still-unfinished building of the City of God, he had to oppose the doctrine claiming it was already complete; in the earthly Church, he had to discern and indicate the unfulfilled but gradually realized divine plan.

3. Since, in the West, the principle of unity was embodied in the Roman Church, the Western apologist of Christian unity was inevitably an apologist for Roman unity, regardless of his personal sympathies or antipathies. As an apologist, he was less a builder than a witness of the building: he did not propose his own plan, but defended the one being realized before his eyes.

Such is the character of Augustine's anti-Donatist apologetics. The salvation of the individual and of society lies in the objective unity of the Church, which does not depend on the personal holiness of its members. The Church cannot be stained by the vices of its ministers; in her earthly imperfection, she is not a society of saints. On the contrary, according to the Gospel, the earthly Church is a net drawing in all kinds of fish, good and evil; a field where tares grow alongside wheat. She embraces many who will not enter the kingdom of the age to come, and excludes many who will. She is the society of saints only in the idea of the coming kingdom; until the Last Judgment, wheat cannot be separated from tares, and the earthly Church remains a mixed body. In short, the earthly, visible Church, in relation to the ideal Church of the age to come, is but an unfinished building. The guardian of this unity is the bishop of Rome, bound by unbroken succession to the chief apostle, Peter; therefore, an anti-Roman church, like the Donatist community, is by that very fact not the true, universal Church.

Such were Augustine's arguments against the Donatists. Thus, for all their difference from the Manicheans, they converge with them in resisting the principle of divine universal organization: the Manicheans in the cosmic order, the Donatists in the social order. The apologist's task against both is essentially the same, and the polemic with Donatists merely continues what was begun against the Manicheans: the unfolding of the theocratic idea of Western Christianity. Against the Manicheans, Augustine defended divine rule as the law of the universe. Against the Donatists, he defended the earthly Church as the earthly realization of this eternal architectural plan in human society, the temporal, imperfect form of divine rule.

CHAPTER: III

Immeasurably more important than the two previous stages is the third stage of Augustine's apologetic activity – his struggle against Pelagianism. For if with the Manicheans the debate concerned the unity of the universe, and with the Donatists the unity of the Church, the Pelagians raised the question of the very principle of the inner religious life of the person and of the social life of the Church – namely, grace. The question of the relationship between grace and human nature and freedom is the question of the very essence of the Church, for the Church, according to its own teaching, is a union of free persons united and organized into one social body by grace. Therefore, the whole sum of her institutions and sacraments, her entire social organization, is itself a concrete relation between grace and freedom – that is, already an answer to the question of grace. At the same time, what is at stake here is the very essence of Christian divine rule – namely, the relation between the two fundamental elements of the divine kingdom: grace and freedom. In another form, this same fatal question, prepared by all the events of that time and sharpened by the fall of Rome, is the question of the social foundations of the new society that must be built on the ruins of the old.

In that disastrous age, under the fresh impression of Alaric's invasion and the sack of the ancient capital, the Christian society of the Latin West first asked itself whence it should expect salvation: from the almighty divine grace manifested in the collective organization of the Church, or from the awakened energy of personal activity? In view of the global crisis, as humanity prepared to enter a new world-historical epoch, it seemed to weigh and test its strength, comparing human freedom and power with the power of God's grace. It naturally asked itself: what can man do with his freedom? Are his powers sufficient to free himself from the sins of the ancient world and to build a renewed society? Or does he need the gracious help of God for the coming rebirth? Is it man or God who must be the builder of the new order?

The struggle between Pelagius and Augustine began in 411, a year after the sack of Rome, precisely in response to these events. In reality, it was a dispute about the social mission and task of the Church; the outcome of which depended on the whole subsequent course of world history. In this dogmatic polemic, the two opponents represent, in theory and dogma, two world-historical principles that were already struggling in society at the time, and from whose interaction medieval

Europe was formed.

The main factor of salvation for Pelagius is the free individual, saved by the personal effort of his will; Augustine's principle, set forth against Pelagius, is almighty grace, of which the ideal embodiment can only be the almighty Church. At first glance, what connection could there be between Pelagian salvation by merit and the world events of that time? What link between Pelagian denial of original sin and the social upheavals of the age? Yet in fact such a connection exists, and it is immediate: for by these two Pelagian doctrines, there is introduced into the basis of religious life an extremely individualistic principle, threatening the overthrow of the whole social edifice of the Church. These two propositions deny the unity of the human race as an organized whole. Humanity is no longer organically bound either in the earthly ancestor Adam or in the spiritual ancestor Christ. The individual stands disconnected from the human race. He is not bound to its past, its history: he is free from the sins of his forebears and cannot transmit his sins or virtues to posterity; he is not bound in solidarity with his neighbors – neither in the present, nor in the past, nor in the hope of the future. We do not sin or die in Adam: Adam's sin harmed him alone, and each of us is individually guilty of his own sin. Likewise, we are not saved or resurrected in Christ by the free grace of God; we are saved by our individual merits: each of us is the individual author of his own salvation. This individualism is the very core of Pelagianism.

The Pelagians did not deny grace as such, but they denied any social action of grace. Just as there is no collective, hereditary sin, so also grace is not a principle of collective organization: Pelagian individualism excludes both the solidarity of mankind in sin and the solidarity of mankind in salvation. They did not deny God's gracious help to man, but for them, grace was not the unified action of the Deity embracing and organizing humanity into one communion. Instead, grace was fragmented into countless individual acts of divine will, conceived as a series of purely external influences upon the isolated individual. These influences were reduced to three main ones: creation, law, and teaching. In creating man, God implanted in him the natural law, giving him free will for its fulfillment. Man could have refrained from sinning, but since he did sin, the natural consciousness of moral law proved insufficient. Hence, the need for an external reminder of revealed law, and ultimately, the external authoritative example and teaching of the Savior. Christ's life and sufferings are His individual merit, not a universal saving act; His death on the cross did not redeem our sins, which were alien to Him. It may save us not as redemption but as instruction and example, encouraging us to keep the law. Man is not organically bound to his Savior but only externally, as disciple and imitator. Each of us may be saved not by another's merits but only by perfectly and flawlessly keeping the law. The principle of salvation is not mercy but God's justice, expressed in the formula "to each his own." Salvation is possible only by perfect observance of the law: those who fail in even one jot fall under merciless condemnation and eternal hell.

It is easy to see the connection between this teaching and the public mood and events of the time. Pelagius, who began preaching in Rome a few years before the catastrophe of 410, was struck by the deep moral decay of Roman society. Facing the looming storm from every side, he deemed it necessary to rouse society from moral sloth, apathy, and despair, to awaken in its sick organism a saving reaction. "Salvation lies in man himself," thought Pelagius. To stir society to action, one must first restore its shaken confidence in its own strength. In one of his letters, he states that the most effective way to encourage people to do good is to give them hope; the most effective preaching, therefore, is that which begins by pointing to the power and might of human nature. The best encouragement for battle is to point out the strength of the army. To make a man work for his salvation, one must convince him that it depends upon himself, that it is in his power. God, in commanding man to keep His law, would not demand the impossible. Clearly, then, He gave us freedom as the necessary means to obey. "Therefore, if we must, then we can," concluded Pelagius – almost in Kantian fashion.

From this perspective, the doctrines of original sin and of grace freely given are nothing but excuses for apathy and laziness. By them, personal responsibility is removed, since our sins are attributed to inherited nature, and salvation appears as a gift of God independent of us. A characteristic of Pelagian doctrine is its denial of any mystical element in Christianity, as well as any supernatural action of God upon man. Law and the free individual who fulfills it – these are the only factors of salvation. Indeed, Pelagianism declares man free from all supernatural influence precisely to bind him more tightly to the external law; it seeks to deprive him of hope in divine mercy, making him more zealous in keeping the law. It leaves the entire system of church institutions untouched, but reduces them to a purely external, juridical mechanism. The saving power lies not in any mystical, regenerating influence on the human will, for the will is not corrupted by original sin and thus needs no rebirth. Salvation is achieved by its own strength; church institutions and sacraments are only obligatory external norms, observance of which determines our salvation.

Remarkably, Pelagius himself, a zealous and strict monk, was motivated in his preaching by ascetic motives. He believed that man is saved by the works of the law and wanted to spur his followers to outward ascetic practices. He attached great importance to the ascetic way of life, but for him, its entire meaning was reduced to keeping the external commandment. Deeds and practical goals came first; he considered dogmatic disputes trivial. The doctrines he proclaimed were not an end but a means to awaken energy in people. A legalist by nature, he least of all wished to be a novator; on the contrary, he regarded himself as a faithful conservative Catholic, a guardian of the law. He strove to present his teaching as the most ancient tradition of the universal Church, supporting it with the authority of the Fathers.

Naturally, Pelagius' preaching was inconsistent and full of contradictions. If man is saved by his natural strength, if the law is implanted in him by nature, then he could just as easily be saved without the artificial external mechanism of the Church. If each of us is born in the state of

Adam before the fall, if human nature in its earthly reality is good, then salvation requires only following our nature and its natural inclinations; the ascetic struggle is then superfluous and useless. Thus, Pelagianism could serve as a justification for worldly attitudes. It produced a secular reaction and intensified it by turning religion and the Church into an absolutely external and alien mechanism; thus, it freed its followers from both the Church and Christianity, inevitably turning into a worldly, humanistic preaching. Pelagius' ascetic teaching indeed passed into the secular Pelagianism of his disciple and follower, the famous Julian of Eclanum. Julian openly declared natural virtue sufficient for salvation: for him, belonging or not belonging to the Church was a matter of indifference.

Pelagius also asserted that the Old Law was just as sufficient for salvation as the Gospel. And Julian, further developing his teacher's idea, concluded that the pagan virtue of some Fabricius was just as saving as the righteousness of Job or righteousness in the Christian sense of the word, and that salvation could be attained just as easily within the Church as outside it. Pelagius the ascetic attached great importance to sexual abstinence. Julian, however, being a more consistent thinker, maintained that if sin is not transmitted through intercourse, then there is nothing sinful in sexual desire; if human nature is good, then in its natural inclinations, there can be nothing blameworthy, and ascetic abstinence is no merit. The characteristic motto of Julian's secular preaching was the formula: "Man, emancipated by God" (Homo a Deo emancipatus). In Julian, in fact, Pelagius' teaching was emancipated from Christianity itself. For Julian, Scripture itself carried authority only insofar as it did not contradict reason; for him, man in his natural state was the highest ideal. Such a view had little in common with Christianity; Julian might instead be called a fifth-century humanist, his doctrine being more pagan than Christian in its wisdom. In all this, the character of Pelagianism is sufficiently exposed as a pagan reaction on church soil. In Pelagian doctrine, especially in Julian, there is undoubtedly a Hellenic philosophical element; but the dominant feature of the teaching – its practical character – is not Hellenic but essentially Latin, Roman.

Pelagianism is the typical embodiment of Roman practical religiosity, in which practical tasks are primary and speculation secondary; in which the supremacy of external law is the absolute goal, and everything else holds only conditional value as a means. This feature has remained one of the typical traits of Roman religious piety to this day; it connects Pelagius with the narrowly clerical orientation that has been strong in the Latin West at all times. The practical nature of Pelagianism shows that the Hellenic philosophical element in it has only secondary significance. By its overall structure and character, Pelagianism is most closely related to Roman paganism. For the most characteristic trait of Roman paganism, as all eminent modern historians have noted, was legal formalism, reducing man's relation to the deity and religion itself to mechanical observance of law, to dead external performance. All religious life in pagan Rome was built on the principle that man is justified before his gods by the performance of specific external actions required by law; that keeping these external prescriptions had saving value regardless of inner disposition, and that the slightest violation was fatal, since divine justice knew no mercy. The deity stood to man as creditor to debtor; man received only the equivalent of his merits and could be saved from wrath only by exact fulfillment of the contract. All these Roman pagan principles were incorporated into Pelagius' teaching, which thus became nothing more than a Latin pagan reaction under the outward shell of Christianity. Exhausted Roman paganism, having lost its own life force, wished to live parasitically, on another's life, grafted onto the Church, and it revived in the form of Pelagius' Christian heresy. Like Roman paganism, Pelagianism viewed religious communion as an assembly of individual atoms united only externally by law and the artificial mechanisms of institutions. It combined Roman juridical universalism with Roman religious individualism, which reduced religion to a private-legal relation. By this, its historical fate was predetermined. Pagan Rome fell apart because it ceased to be a living organism, remaining only an artificial mechanical aggregation. And surely Pelagianism, with its individualist worldview, could not reassemble and raise anew the crumbled structure. In essence, Pelagian teaching said: "Save yourselves, whoever can and however you can."

Clearly, the Church could not oppose the barbarians with such Pelagian sauve qui peut. To triumph over Germanic individualism, it first had to subdue this Pelagian, Latin individualism that had arisen in its midst. The whole course of world history would have been different if the Church, rejecting Augustine, had followed Pelagius. In reality, it condemned Pelagius and entered the barbarian Germanic world as a united, organized force, one that organized and unified. With Augustine, salvation was recognized as an everyday, social act, not as an individual act of human will; it acknowledged the saving, mystical action of grace, not the abstract freedom of the individual. And with this principle, it indeed saved world civilization from collapse and ruin, restrained the barbarians, and opened a new field for the spread of Christian and classical culture.

All the events of that time suggest that, by his natural powers, man cannot be saved; that Rome's salvation from the barbarians could only be a miracle of God's grace. At the very moment when the Latin world awaited and demanded this manifestation of divine power and authority, Augustine appeared as the apologist of grace – that is, of the Christian apologetic principle against Pelagius' individualist worldview.

Augustine's teaching, in contrast to his opponents' self-confident preaching, began from the humble recognition of human weakness, of man's impotence for good. It rested on observation of human nature in general and of contemporary society in particular. It was thereby justified far more than Pelagius' view, which rested only on a speculative presupposition – an abstract concept of a human personality absolutely free, such as had never been observed in experience.

Behind Augustine stood the whole historical experience of a society that had painfully tested its impotence. He believed in the power of God, perfected in the humility of the human will; he was convinced that man cannot earn his salvation, and preached salvation as a gift, an act of God's mercy and grace, without any preceding human merits. The so-called merits of which we boast are only the result of this divine gift, without which no movement of our will toward good is possible. God not only gives us the command, but also moves our will to fulfill it. This relation of the human will to grace is most vividly expressed in Augustine's famous prayer, which scandalized Pelagius: "Give us what You command, and command what You will." Not only our deeds, but even our faith itself, both in its origin and its growth, is the work of grace. "God works marvelously in our hearts, so that we believe." He not only gives us the power to do good, but also produces in us the very desire for good. He anticipates our will in its movement toward good. We need the help of grace in every good action; without it, we do nothing good. Grace accompanies us from cradle to grave, extending to every step of our spiritual life, enlightening our mind and heart from within, edifying and aiding us from without, preceding our spiritual life and following it in the process of our gradual growth. This action of grace cannot be exhausted by any external manifestations, being in essence mysterious and mystical.

By grace, Augustine essentially understood

that mysterious fact in which God imparts Himself to man, the action of the indivisible Trinity upon the mind and will of man. For the Father instructs and teaches us inwardly, so that we may come to the Son and be filled with the Spirit and with love. This gracious action is not a relation between God and the isolated individual. However, it is by its very nature social, having as its object mankind as a race, as a society. Man is not left to himself in the work of salvation, but is bound in solidarity with the human race. He is connected with his fellows by a natural tie through the common ancestor Adam, and thus by a common bond of sin. Adam, for Augustine, is the embodiment of our common social nature, and Adam's sin is therefore not only an act of an individual will, but a racial, social fact. "We were all in him, when we were all he alone." We did not yet exist as individuals, but we already existed as nature, in the seed of our ancestor, and inherited from him a sinful constitution. Second, the individual is bound to humanity by the bond of grace, which unites all participants in salvation into a single social whole through their common spiritual ancestor, Christ. The ideal goal of the process of grace is that all the elect be one body of Christ, or, as Augustine put it, one Christ. To collective sin there is opposed the collective action of grace upon mankind as a race, as a single organism. Augustine himself said of this teaching on grace that he had to develop it against the Pelagians; before this heresy, which denied grace, there had been no need of such a theological theory. For the Church itself, by its actions, prayers, and sacraments, bore witness to what it understood by grace. The whole Lord's Prayer could be summed up in the words: "Give what You command"; and the Church's practice of baptizing infants "for the remission of sins" testified to original sin, to which they were subject, since it was impossible to suppose in infants an individual sin. The elementary earthly form of grace's action, for Augustine, is the social life of the earthly Church; its ultimate, absolute goal is the social unity of the elect in Christ, the unity of the eternal City of God.

CHAPTER: IV

Thus, as is clear from all that has been said above, the entire apologetic activity of Augustine is permeated by one central idea and one historical motive. Theocracy, as the law of the universe, as the principle of the architectural unity of the Church, as the content of the religious life of the individual and of society – these are the three stages of his work, which are all summed up in two words: Civitas Dei. But we must not forget the cultural-historical task that fell to the great Father of the Church.

The central world-historical task of Western Christianity at that time was to secure Latin unity against the barbarians. This unity, which had to be preserved and defended at all costs, was not only Christian and ecclesiastical, but also secular and political. As we have already pointed out, the Western Church then bore the burden of secular society on its shoulders. State unity rested solely upon it; ecclesiastical and worldly relations were so closely intertwined that no one could say where the state began and the church ended. The Western apologist of Christian unity was, therefore, willingly or unwillingly, also the apologist of Latin unity; his teaching was not pure, unmixed Christianity: his ideal was inevitably saturated with secular and political traditions. Consciously or unconsciously, he took part in building the new Christian Rome, in which the old, pagan Rome still made itself felt. His ideal of the eternal City of God was the direct antithesis of the pagan eternal city, an ideal anti-Rome. Augustine was not the apologist of pure Christianity, but of its Western, one-sided form. The Latin ideal, threatened by the barbarian world, was above all the ideal of universal law, of a universal world order. To overcome the barbarians, an irresistible, superhuman law had to be opposed to them.

The concept of a universal divine law, realized in all things and governing all, is indeed the central concept of Augustine's worldview, as will be demonstrated below. Against the Manichaeans, who divided the universe into two kingdoms, he defended the principle of divine monarchy in the cosmic order. But what here serves as the supreme expression of divine power? Not love, by which God draws all to Himself and reconciles all with Himself, but law, by which He orders all things from eternity, the single order by which He regulates everything. The single order is the highest manifestation of divine authority, the beginning and end of all being. From Augustine's theodicy, suffering and destruction are indifferent facts, since no creature can disturb the order of creation. The triumph of law is equally expressed in the victory of good and in the punishment of evil; indeed, evil is a necessary antithesis to good, for through it, as through shadow in a painting, the light stands out more sharply and clearly.

The Christian principle of divine love, for which every creature is precious, is by no means the central idea of Augustine's teaching. His supreme principle is not love, but order, law, which guards even those who resist it. Love, in this view, is not God's relation to creation in general, but only a partial manifestation of the eternal divine order. Another characteristic is Augustine's relation to the mystery of the Incarnation. This central principle of Christianity is treated by him only as one moment in the world order. The incarnation of God is not the absolute end, but only a means to the restoration of law disrupted by human sin. Its purpose lies not in itself, but partly in satisfying divine justice, partly in educating the human race, which can perceive divine order only in sensory form. Thus, the central principle of Christianity in Augustine is reduced to a particular incident caused by human sin.

Against the dualism of the Manichaeans, he advanced the Latin theocratic principle as the almighty eternal law, in relation to which the humanity of the Deity had only the subordinate value of a means. Equally Latin in character is the defense of church unity he advanced against the Donatists. The essence of their dispute was such that the apologist of church unity inevitably became also the apologist of political unity. For if Donatism was the uprising of African nationalism against the universal Roman idea in both the Church and the state, then the universal Church stood against the Donatists as the representative of the idea of a universal legal order. In this struggle, the Church appeared to Augustine as a legal organism wielding the force of the secular sword against heretics, as a coercive and compulsory unity.

Augustine himself at first opposed coercion. "My original opinion," he writes, "was that no one should be compelled to the unity of Christ; that it was necessary to act with words, to contend with arguments, to conquer with reason, so as not to make false Catholics of those whom we knew as open heretics." Thus, Augustine reasoned as late as 404 at the Council of Carthage. A deeply religious thinker, he desired an intimate, inward union with God, not an external, coercive one. But he saw the Roman, and predominantly African, society of his day, which could hardly be swayed by persuasion or preaching; such a society could be overcome only by fear and force. Beholding in it the abyss of perverted human nature, the great apologist saw that in its present sinful condition, the mass of people could be compelled to good only by force. Accordingly, Christ's unity for the great majority had inevitably to be an external, coercive unity. Meanwhile, to save a disintegrating society, it was necessary to confine it within the Church's enclosure. Unity was required at all costs, and if it could not be achieved by the spiritual sword, recourse had to be had to the secular one.

Before Augustine's eyes, the state indeed took up the conversion of heretics, and with success. After the Council of Carthage in 404 (and at the petition of that same council, where Augustine's liberal opinion did not prevail) came the harsh edicts of Emperor Honorius, which began the real persecution of the Donatists. And now, under the influence of these coercive measures, the Donatists began to pass en masse into the dominant Church. "We see that not just certain individuals, but whole cities which before were Donatist, have now become Catholic," Augustine wrote in 408. "They hate the devil's division and ardently love unity"; they "became Catholic because of the imperial laws." Under the influence of these events, Augustine renounced his earlier opinion, refuting in 408 what he had preached in 404. The futility of his former view, he said, was now revealed not by the arguments of his opponents but by facts themselves, by living examples. Thus, the city of Hippo, where Augustine was bishop and which, before the edicts, was almost entirely Donatist, was by them converted to Catholicism.

Augustine was far more the apologist of an objective historical system than the preacher of his personal religious views. The unity of the universal divine order was his ideal, and before his eyes it was realized through coercion and force. Now he saw in compulsory secular measures against heretics a necessary, providential fact. God's action upon our perverted nature must inevitably be violent. "Who can love us more than God!" Augustine exclaims, "and yet He ceases not only to teach us kindly, but also to frighten us profitably." God Himself uses coercion, as is seen in the example of the apostle Paul, "who was compelled to the knowledge and possession of the truth by the great violence of Christ." God prescribes coercion, as is seen in the parable of the householder who, sending his servant to call guests to supper, tells him: "Compel them to come in" (Luke 14:23).

Given the mingling of ecclesiastical and political order characteristic of that epoch, it is not surprising that Augustine confuses the gracious order with the legal order, and secular coercion is taken by him as the necessary mode of grace's action. From the fact that God frightens and punishes, his theory directly concludes that the state must frighten and punish heretics, i.e., perform pastoral duties. On the other hand, spiritual authority itself is invested with the power and might of state authority, for "the shepherd must sometimes with his rod bring back the stray sheep to the flock." Heresy he classifies with common criminal offenses: if the state punishes thieves and counterfeiters, how much more should it punish heretics! Thus, in his polemic with the Donatists, the juridical, Latin element triumphed over Augustine's personal religious sentiment, and he became, willingly or unwillingly, the apologist of the church-state against the anti-church and anti-state movement of the Donatists.

This Latin element is no less evident in the anti-Pelagian preaching of the great Father of the Church. Human nature is crushed by the power of evil, and human freedom is only a negative, evil principle: such was Augustine's central conviction, the fruit of lifelong observation and experience. Naturally, then, good appeared to him only as an absolutely superhuman principle, and he understood grace as fatum, accomplishing man's salvation by destroying his freedom. By the essence of the fundamental Christian principle, salvation cannot be the work of God alone nor of man alone.

The Christian idea of the God-man requires, besides the gracious action from above, also the cooperation of human freedom in the work of salvation. But humanity, as Augustine observed, was neither healthy nor normal, and it is not surprising that salvation appeared to him as a one-sided action of grace, in which the human element had only a passive role. The principle of freedom in that decayed society was centrifugal and destructive, and in Pelagianism, its real relation to the social order of the time was revealed. The principle of freedom in Pelagian doctrine was expressed just as it was in the historical reality of the age, in the denial of organic social unity and in rebellion against the mystical, organizing action of grace. For the salvation of society, this destructive principle had to be forcibly curbed and suppressed: the collective unity of the church organism for the masses could be only coercive and compulsory. Herein lie the peculiar features of Augustine's teaching on grace.

The grace of God appeared to him as an almighty, irresistible power. It created the spiritual strength of Rome with the hands of barbarians who destroyed its temporal power; it brought men to unity in Christ by the force of the secular sword; it triumphed in the fall and abasement of human strength, sent calamities upon men for their correction, acted upon them with shocks and blows; it shook the foundations of the universe and accomplished the miracle of human salvation by crushing, compelling, and destroying. In relation to the society of that time, Christianity was only in name but pagan in essence; it was an external, violent law, stern and inexorable, for it was its condemnation and abolition; in relation to that society, it was fatum. Such indeed grace must have appeared to Christians of that time. But Augustine took this temporary manifestation of grace as the universal law of its action. "The predestination of God about good," he says, "is the preparation of grace, and grace is the consequence of predestination itself." Moreover, predestination, this eternal law by which God has ordered all things, is, from Augustine's point of view, God's universal relation to creation, while grace is only its particular action. Predestination is the universal law realized in the whole structure of the cosmos, both in the salvation of the righteous and in the condemnation of the wicked: it extends to all. Grace, however, saves only some, the elect, those predestined to be saved. Its sphere of action is limited: it relates to predestination as the particular to the universal. Both the salvation and the condemnation of men have from eternity been accomplished in predestination.

From this point of view, of course, one cannot speak of any free cooperation of man in the work of salvation. Every movement of the human will toward the good is merely an automatic repetition of the eternal divine act; grace, saving by predestination, is the complete negation of freedom. In this lies the great imperfection of Augustine's teaching.

If we adopt a conditional historical perspective, we must acknowledge that, in relation to his historical context and era, he was correct. The great world-historical crisis unfolding before his eyes was indeed a great violence of Christ against sinful humanity, and thus the triumph of Augustinian principles and the defeat of Pelagianism. But for a complete historical evaluation of a doctrine that, above all, seeks to be Christian, it is necessary to clarify its relation to Christianity as a whole. If we examine it from a universal Christian perspective, we can easily see that it contains a certain deviation from the fundamental Christian principle. As we observed earlier, when characterizing Augustine's anti-Manichaean works, the central idea of Christianity – the Incarnation – is not the central principle of his teaching. The same must be said of his anti-Pelagian preaching. Here, too, the fundamental concept is eternal order, law acting as predestination, rather than the God-man person of Christ.

According to Augustine, Christ is the highest manifestation of grace: in Him, "as in our Head, the very source of grace is revealed, from which it flows to all the members of His body." Christ is a man assumed by the Word of God and made one with Him without any preceding merits. The highest manifestation of the gracious principle, Christ, is therefore the highest manifestation of predestination. "Is there a more glorious example of predestination than Jesus Himself?" "Whoever among the faithful wants to understand predestination rightly should look to Him and in Him will find himself." God, who made this man of David's seed, assumed by Him, righteous without any preceding merits, will act likewise with the saints whom He has predestined. God in men, as in Him, produces goodwill. The Creator of the universe "predestined both Him and us. For in Him, that He should become our Head, and in us, that we should become His members, He foresaw not our deeds that were to precede, but His future works." Thus Christ's human will, like the human will in general, is reduced by Augustine to a passive medium of grace, an automatic instrument of predestination. And since grace itself is not the universal divine action, but only one of the consequences of predestination, the humanity of Christ, as the chief expression of grace, is only a particular manifestation of the universal law of predestination.

This Christology of Augustine is the best indicator of the relationship between his theocratic ideal and the Christian idea. The Christian ideal requires the perfect reconciliation of human freedom with divine grace in Christ – an organic unity and cooperation of the free Deity and free humanity. Meanwhile, Augustine's teaching fundamentally denies human freedom in Christ. Of course, even from the standpoint of the universal Christian idea, our sinful condition is a state of relative unfreedom. However, Augustine's teaching elevates this relative, temporary state into an eternal and absolute principle; precisely in this lies its deviation from Christian teachings.

The highest concept in Augustine's teaching is the divine order of the universe; the universal rule of divine law is his social ideal. This ideal of universal divine law and justice as the universal norm of social relations is indeed a necessary element of Christianity. But Augustine's error lies in the fact that he took a part for the whole, one aspect of Christianity for all of Christianity, and elevated one of its moments to the supreme principle. This error, however, is not a purely personal mistake of the great Father of the Church, but a feature of that one-sided form of Christianity which he represents.

As noted above, Augustine is the apologist of the Latin idea in Christianity, and insofar as he accepts this Latin element as the highest and absolute, he inevitably deviates into Roman paganism, yielding to the force of centuries-old tradition of the Latin West. Here, he meets his opponent Pelagius, with whom, despite all their disagreements and differences, he stands on common historical ground. Despite the profound contrast in their way of thinking, in their direction and character, despite the immeasurable superiority of the great Father of the Church over the heretic condemned by the Church, in both men, one can easily recognize the common family traits of the Latin type. Ultimately, both preach salvation through the law; both elevate the law to an absolute principle. But for Pelagius, the supreme principle is law as an external empirical norm, on the observance of which salvation depends.

In contrast, for Augustine, the supreme principle is the eternal divine law as predestination. The fundamental difference between the two lies in this: for Pelagius, the executor of the law is free human will, rewarded for its merits; for Augustine, it is grace acting by predestination. The one attributes salvation to the unilateral action of man, the other to that of God. In both, the legalistic element of the doctrine expresses itself in the diminishment of the God-man person of Christ. For if for Pelagius the life and suffering of Christ is only His private merit before the law, devoid of universal significance, then for Augustine likewise the humanity of Christ, as we have seen, is only a particular manifestation of the eternal law, and the social action of grace is limited in scope.

Pelagianism contains one side of the Christian theocratic ideal that Augustine lacks: this ideal truly requires a human will capable of co-operating with grace in freedom. From this point of view, Pelagius is right in emphasizing human freedom of action; however, his teaching is anti-Christian and anti-theocratic insofar as it affirms freedom in a one-sided manner, severing human will from the social, organizing action of grace. Christian theocracy does not want to be a work of human hands, and from this perspective, Pelagius is wrong. But on the other hand, Augustine, representing the opposite one-sidedness, is just as right and just as wrong as his opponents, the Pelagians.

Christian theocracy does not want to be the work of God alone; it also requires free humanity as the basis for the action of grace. As a one-sided doctrine, Augustinianism could never overcome its opposite one-sidedness, Pelagianism, which always stands opposed to it with a certain, albeit lesser, historical right. But apart from the relative correctness of Augustinianism, as a doctrine more in accord with the ideal historical demands and events of that epoch, it has yet another enormous advantage. Pelagianism, as an individualistic, anti-church worldview, was not restrained in its development by church tradition, which indeed soon definitively rejected it. The individual was left to his own judgment and whim; hence, Pelagianism quickly broke away from Christianity, revealing its pagan features. Augustine stood in another position. As the apologist of the social life of the Church and of ecclesiastical organization, he was more restrained in his preaching.

Meanwhile, although by then the characteristics of the two halves of Christianity – Eastern, Hellenic, and Western, Latin – had already become pronounced, they had not yet begun their fratricidal quarrel. These characteristics, therefore, were moderated and restrained by the common universal-Christian principles on which the worldwide Christian union was established and maintained. The beneficial and saving actions of these principles were expressed in the daily life of the churches and in the works of Christian thinkers; they were also reflected in Augustine's teachings. The Latin element of this teaching is moderated and restrained not only by the immense richness of Christian ideas it contains, but also by his deeply Christian personal disposition.

The profoundly religious genius of Augustine, as we have seen, rose and was indignant against violence: he passionately desired freedom, yet was compelled to defend a system founded on the suppression of freedom and on coercion. This system was not his personal invention – it was imposed upon him by history. He struggled with it, and this struggle found expression in numerous hesitations, inconsistencies, and subjective contradictions. In the end, this objective-historical force broke and subdued him, forcing him into the framework of the Latin system and, against his will, making him its father and propagator. Augustine, of course, was not only the apologist of Latinism: he also immortalized his Christian disposition in an excellent, imperishable depiction. The peculiarity of this religious disposition is such that it does not fit into any systematic framework. For Augustine, the religious life of the individual is above all the intimate, immediate relation of man to God, characterized by the words "to live in God," "to cling to God."

In his Confessions, Augustine describes the process of religious seeking, which finds rest only in the perfect certainty of possessing God. Fervent love of God combined with deep awareness of human sinfulness, trust in Him, and hope for forgiveness – such are the fundamental motives of this disposition, deeply religious and deeply Christian. However, this Christian element of Augustine's personal disposition does not fully harmonize with his system and partly stands in direct contradiction to it. In essence, it is undermined by the system at its very root. For if the supreme principle of the relation of God to creation is not love, but an impassive, cold law that renders to each his due; if the saving action of grace is limited to a minority of predestined elect; if, finally, the Son of God is redemption not for all but only for some – then no one can be assured of his salvation. Then there can be no talk of trust in God, and man's relation to Him becomes one of eternal fear, which hope cannot balance. From the standpoint of "order," the condemnation or salvation of a person is an indifferent fact; the individual is not an end, but is deprived of absolute worth and significance. Augustine's system, therefore, does not provide sufficient objective grounds for religious hope and does not give the repose in God that his disposition seeks. That is why Augustine is far more sympathetic in his Confessions than in his doctrine; he is more attractive in what he sought than in what he found.

Printed in Dunstable, United Kingdom